GILLES DELEUZE

'This book is that rare thing, an introduction to the work of a complex thinker that actually does what it is supposed to do: it shows you how to use Deleuze's thought to do new things. Students will find this to be an excellent starting point.'

Ian Buchanan, *University of Tasmania*

'A remarkably lucid and insightful overview of the thought of Gilles Deleuze, especially successful in drawing out the implications of Deleuze's philosophy for literary analysis. Readers new to Deleuze will find in this volume a friendly and reliable guide.'

Ronald Bogue, *University of Georgia*

'This would be an ideal starting point for anyone approaching Deleuze's work for the first time.'

Mary Bryden, *University of Reading*

This book provides a comprehensive introduction to one of the twentieth century's most exciting and challenging intellectuals, Gilles Deleuze. Deleuze's writings covered literature, art, psychoanalysis, philosophy, genetics, film and social theory. He also created a whole new style of thought and writing, insisting that new modes of thought are capable of transforming life. In this volume, Claire Colebrook reads Deleuze's work according to his own stated aims and problems: the problems of creation, the future and the enhancement of life.

As well as introducing Deleuze's concepts and ideas, *Gilles Deleuze* shows students how his work can provide new readings of literary texts. This, then, is the essential guide to Deleuze for any student of literature.

Claire Colebrook teaches English Literature at the University of Edinburgh. She is the author of *New Literary Histories* (1997) and *Ethics and Representation* (1999). She has also published on Derrida, Heidegger, Irigaray, Blake and Foucault.

ROUTLEDGE CRITICAL THINKERS

Series Editor: Robert Eaglestone, Royal Holloway, University of London

Routledge Critical Thinkers is a series of accessible introductions to key figures in contemporary critical thought.

With a unique focus on historical and intellectual contexts, each volume examines a key theorist's:

- significance
- motivation
- key ideas and their sources
- impact on other thinkers

Concluding with extensively annotated guides to further reading, *Routledge Critical Thinkers* are the student's passport to today's most exciting critical thought.

Already available:

Jean Baudrillard by Richard J. Lane
Maurice Blanchot by Ullrich Haase and William Large
Judith Butler by Sara Salih
Sigmund Freud by Pamela Thurschwell
Martin Heidegger by Timothy Clark
Fredric Jameson by Adam Roberts
Paul de Man by Martin McQuillan
Edward Said by Bill Ashcroft and Pal Ahluwalia

For further details on this series, see www.literature.routledge.com/rct

GILLES DELEUZE

Claire Colebrook

Routledge
Taylor & Francis Group

LONDON AND NEW YORK

First published 2002
by Routledge
2 Park Square, Milton Park, Abingdon, Oxon OX14 4RN

Simultaneously published in the USA and Canada
by Routledge
270 Madison Ave, New York, NY 10016

Reprinted 2002, 2003, 2005 (twice), 2006, 2007, 2008

Transferred to Digital Printing 2008

Routledge is an imprint of the Taylor & Francis Group, an informa business

© 2002 Claire Colebrook

Typeset in Perpetua by Florence Production Ltd, Stoodleigh, Devon
Printed and bound in Great Britain by TJI Digital, Padstow, Cornwall

British Library Cataloguing in Publication Data
A catalogue record for this book is available from the British Library.

Library of Congress Cataloging in Publication Data
Colebrook, Claire.
  Gilles Deleuze/Claire Colebrook
    p. cm. – (Routledge critical thinkers)
  Includes bibliographical references and index.
  1. Deleuze, Gilles. I. Title. II. Series.

B2430.D454 C65 2001
194–dc21   2001019897

ISBN10 0–415–24633–4 (hbk)
ISBN10 0–415–24634–2 (pbk)

ISBN13 978–0–415–24633–0 (hbk)
ISBN13 978–0–415–24634–7 (pbk)

CONTENTS

SERIES EDITOR'S PREFACE

The books in this series offer introductions to major critical thinkers who have influenced literary studies and the humanities. The *Routledge Critical Thinkers* series provides the books you can turn to first when a new name or concept appears in your studies.

Each book will equip you to approach a key thinker's original texts by explaining her or his key ideas, putting them into context and, perhaps most importantly, showing you why this thinker is considered to be significant. The emphasis is on concise, clearly written guides which do not presuppose a specialist knowledge. Although the focus is on particular figures, the series stresses that no critical thinker ever existed in a vacuum but, instead, emerged from a broader intellectual, cultural and social history. Finally, these books will act as a bridge between you and the thinker's original texts: not replacing them but rather complementing what she or he wrote.

These books are necessary for a number of reasons. In his 1997 autobiography, *Not Entitled*, the literary critic Frank Kermode wrote of a time in the 1960s:

> On beautiful summer lawns, young people lay together all night, recovering from their daytime exertions and listening to a troupe of Balinese musicians. Under their blankets or their sleeping bags, they would chat drowsily about the gurus of the time. . . . What they repeated was largely hearsay; hence my

lunchtime suggestion, quite impromptu, for a series of short, very cheap books
offering authoritative but intelligible introductions to such figures.

There is still a need for 'authoritative and intelligible introductions'.
But this series reflects a different world from the 1960s. New thinkers
have emerged and the reputations of others have risen and fallen, as
new research has developed. New methodologies and challenging ideas
have spread through the arts and humanities. The study of literature
is no longer – if it ever was – simply the study and evaluation of
poems, novels and plays. It is also the study of the ideas, issues, and
difficulties which arise in any literary text and in its interpretation.
Other arts and humanities subjects have changed in analogous ways.

With these changes, new problems have emerged. The ideas and
issues behind these radical changes in the humanities are often
presented without reference to wider contexts or as theories which
you can simply 'add on' to the texts you read. Certainly, there's
nothing wrong with picking out selected ideas or using what comes to
hand – indeed, some thinkers have argued that this is, in fact, all we
can do. However, it is sometimes forgotten that each new idea comes
from the pattern and development of somebody's thought and it is
important to study the range and context of their ideas. Against theories 'floating in space', the *Routledge Critical Thinkers* series places key
thinkers and their ideas firmly back in their contexts.

More than this, these books reflect the need to go back to the
thinker's own texts and ideas. Every interpretation of an idea, even the
most seemingly innocent one, offers its own 'spin', implicitly or
explicitly. To read only books on a thinker, rather than texts by that
thinker, is to deny yourself a chance of making up your own mind.
Sometimes what makes a significant figure's work hard to approach
is not so much its style or content as the feeling of not knowing where
to start. The purpose of these books is to give you a 'way in' by offering an accessible overview of a these thinkers' ideas and works and
by guiding your further reading, starting with each thinker's own
texts. To use a metaphor from the philosopher Ludwig Wittgenstein
(1889–1951), these books are ladders, to be thrown away after you have
climbed to the next level. Not only, then, do they equip you to approach
new ideas, but also they empower you, by leading you back to a theorist's own texts and encouraging you to develop your own informed
opinions.

Finally, these books are necessary because, just as intellectual needs have changed, the education systems around the world – the contexts in which introductory books are usually read – have changed radically, too. What was suitable for the minority higher education system of the 1960s is not suitable for the larger, wider, more diverse, high technology education systems of the 21st century. These changes call not just for new, up-to-date, introductions but new methods of presentation. The presentational aspects of *Routledge Critical Thinkers* have been developed with today's students in mind.

Each book in the series has a similar structure. They begin with a section offering an overview of the life and ideas of each thinker and explain why she or he is important. The central section of each book discusses the thinker's key ideas, their context, evolution and reception. Each book concludes with a survey of the thinker's impact, outlining how their ideas have been taken up and developed by others. In addition, there is a detailed final section suggesting and describing books for further reading. This is not a 'tacked-on' section but an integral part of each volume. In the first part of this section you will find brief descriptions of the thinker's key works: following this, information on the most useful critical works and, in some cases, on relevant websites. This section will guide you in your reading, enabling you to follow your interests and develop your own projects. Throughout each book, references are given in what is known as the Harvard system (the author and the date of works cited are given in the text and you can look up the full details in the bibliography at the back). This offers a lot of information in very little space. The books also explain technical terms and use boxes to describe events or ideas in more detail, away from the main emphasis of the discussion. Boxes are also used at times to highlight definitions of terms frequently used or coined by a thinker. In this way, the boxes serve as a kind of glossary, easily identified when flicking through the book.

The thinkers in the series are 'critical' for three reasons. First, they are examined in the light of subjects which involve criticism: principally literary studies or English and cultural studies, but also other disciplines which rely on the criticism of books, ideas, theories and unquestioned assumptions. Second, they are critical because studying their work will provide you with a 'tool kit' for your own informed critical reading and thought, which will make you critical. Third, these thinkers are critical because they are crucially important: they deal

with ideas and questions which can overturn conventional understandings of the world, of texts, of everything we take for granted,
leaving us with a deeper understanding of what we already knew and
with new ideas.

No introduction can tell you everything. However, by offering a way
into critical thinking, this series hopes to begin to engage you in an
activity which is productive, constructive and potentially life-changing.

ACKNOWLEDGEMENTS

I would like to thank the following people: Liz Grosz and Ian Buchanan for introducing me to Deleuze, Diane Elam, Bob Eaglestone and Liz Thompson for instigating this specific project, Sue Loukomitis, Andrew Lynn and Alan Nicholson for reading drafts of the manuscripts, and the staff and students of Monash University for all their support and encouragement.

WHY DELEUZE?

Why Deleuze? In many ways this is a question Gilles Deleuze (1925–95) himself might have asked. Deleuze took nothing for granted and insisted that the power of life – all life and not just human life – was its power to develop problems. Life poses problems – not just to thinking beings, but to all life. Organisms, cells, machines and sound waves are all responses to the complication or 'problematising' force of life. The questions of philosophy, art and science are extensions of the *questioning power of life*, a power that is also expressed in smaller organisms and their tendency to evolve, mutate and *become*. Deleuze's insistence on becoming is typical of the post-structuralist trend in late twentieth-century thought. Post-structuralist philosophers and thinkers, such as Jacques Derrida and Michel Foucault, did not form a self-conscious group. In different ways they all responded to the twentieth-century events of phenomenology and structuralism. Phenomenology, associated with two German philosophers Edmund Husserl (1859–1938) and Martin Heidegger (1889–1976), rejected previous systems of knowledge and strove to examine life just as it appears (as phenomena). Structuralism, usually associated with the linguist Ferdinand de Saussure (1857–1913), was another twentieth-century movement that attempted to study social systems and languages in a scientific and rigorous manner. Both movements rejected the idea that knowledge could be centred on 'man' or the human knower; both sought to provide a more secure foundation. For phenomenology, such a foundation would be experience itself, without any presuppositions as to who or what was doing the experiencing. For structuralism, knowledge ought not to be founded on experience but on the structures that make experience possible: structures of concepts, language or signs. Structuralists insisted that nothing is meaningful in itself; meaning is determined *in relation* to other components of a system, so that a word has no sense outside of its language. *Post*-structuralism responded to the impossibility of founding knowledge either on pure experience (phenomenology) or systematic structures (structuralism). In Deleuze's case, like many other post-structuralists, this recognised impossibility of organising life into closed structures was not a failure or loss but a cause for celebration and liberation. The fact that we cannot secure a foundation for knowledge means that we are given the opportunity to invent, create and experiment. Deleuze asks us to grasp this opportunity, to accept the challenge to *transform life*.

But why is it that we cannot have such a foundation for knowledge? Why is it that neither experience (phenomenology) nor language (structuralism) provide us with some sort of ground? The problem with appealing to experience, for Deleuze, was that we tend to assume some normative or standard model of experience, such as the human experience of an outside world. We have to ignore *inhuman* experience (such as the experience of animals, nonorganic life and even future experiences of which we have no current image). The problem with basing knowledge on structures was that any attempt to describe such a structure would have to pretend to be outside or above structures. (Structuralist anthropologists did just that: they viewed other cultures to describe their structures, but never asked how their own position of knowledge was structured.) If we want to understand the structure of our language we will still have to use some sort of language to explain it. Even the term 'language' already relies on a structure of distinctions: we can imagine a culture that has no general term for language but might refer to 'signs' or 'symbols'. Deleuze's great problem and contribution was his insistence, in opposition to structuralism, on difference and becoming.

Not only structualism, but the history of Western thought had been based on being and identity. We have always imagined that there is some *being* that then goes through becoming or is then differentiated. Structuralism and phenomenology both placed difference and becoming *within* some ground or foundation: either the structure of language or the point of view of experience. Post-structuralists, in general, rejected the idea that we could examine a static structure of differences that might give us some point of foundation for knowing the world. Post-structuralism sought to explain the emergence, becoming or genesis of structures: how systems such as language both come into being *and* how they mutate through time. For this reason, Deleuze and those of his generation sought to conceptualise both difference and becoming, but a difference and becoming that would not be the becoming *of* some being. Their main target was not just the recent movements of phenomenology and structuralism but the entire history of Western thought. In the 1940s and 1950s the French philosophical scene was dominated by the re-reading of the German philosopher G. W. F. Hegel (1770–1831), who argued that the becoming and difference of life and history could (and should) be comprehended within one single movement of spirit. Hegel also argued that modern philosophy was the end-point of history, the point at which consciousness or spirit could overcome all difference and becoming. Most post-structuralists saw Hegel as typical of the Western suppression of difference, the tendency to reduce difference to some grounding identity. Deleuze differed from his contemporaries regarding the unity of Western thought. He argued that there were many philosophers and thinkers who challenged the Western commitment to some ultimate being and presence. For this reason, his career began with a re-reading of the philosophical tradition. He took quite traditional figures and argued that their works harboured a far more radical potential. His early book on the Scottish Enlightenment philosopher David Hume – published in 1953 when Deleuze was only 28 – argued that the human subject and its stable outside world was a *fiction* produced within the flow of experience: 'the world (continuity and distinction) is an outright fiction of the imagination' (Deleuze 1991, 80). In arguing for the image of the subject and the world as products of the imagination, Deleuze already showed a tendency to interpret philosophy creatively *and* to argue that there was a creative tendency in life itself: the tendency for human life to form images of itself, such as the image of the rational mind or 'subject'.

Instead of studying life in closed systems, as the structuralists had done, post-structuralists looked at the opening, excess or instability of systems: the way languages, organisms, cultures and political systems necessarily mutate or *become*. Indeed, for Deleuze the challenge of thought and writing is the *diversity of becoming*, so that the becoming of a language, for example, can be infected by other modes of becoming such as the becoming of organisms or social systems. (Think of the way our language has changed because of the inventions of science; we use terms from computer science, such as hard-wiring, to describe the brain and terms from genetics, such as viruses, to describe the computer.) Becoming is a Deleuzean *concept*: not just another word but a problem, and for this reason Deleuze will try to give as many nuances and senses to becoming as possible. Both difference and becoming will recur throughout this book in varied and related uses. This is crucial to Deleuze's approach. Instead of providing yet one more system of terms and ideas Deleuze wanted to express the dynamism and instability of thought. He reinvented his style and vocabulary with each project. No term in his work is capable of being defined in itself; any single term makes sense only in its relation to the whole which it helps to create. For this reason reading Deleuze is not an easy task; it is certainly not a question of adding one proposition to another. Rather, you have to begin by seeing the *problem* of Deleuze's work: whether we can *think* difference and becoming without relying on common sense notions of identity, reason, the human subject or even 'being'. Then, you have to read each Deleuzean term and idea as a challenge to think differently. The 'difficulty' of Deleuze is tactical; his works attempt to capture (but not completely) the chaos of life. By the 'end' of this book you should be capable of understanding the beginning, but also of moving beyond the beginning. For *no* system or vocabulary is adequate to represent the flow of life. Indeed, the aim of writing should not be representation but invention.

Like other post-structuralists Deleuze was never a 'pure' philosopher, for if we accept that life is never composed of closed systems then *all* aspects of life will be in a condition of ever-renewing difference and change. Organisms *live* only by responding to other changing systems, such as the environment and other organisms. Similarly, acts of thought, such as philosophy and literature, are also active responses to life. For this reason, Deleuze's philosophy crossed over into reflections on mathematics, art, literature, history, politics and evolutionary theory. Most importantly, Deleuze spent a lot of his career co-authoring works with the French psychoanalyst Félix Guattari (1930–92). It was Deleuze and Guattari's *L'Anti-Oedipe* (published in French in 1972 and translated as *Anti-Oedipus* in 1977) that, until recently, accounted for most of Deleuze's reputation in the English-speaking world. His earlier works were more conventionally philosophical, but *Anti-Oedipus* put forward provocative claims that shattered the usual standards for theory and rational argument. *Anti-Oedipus* followed on from, and extended, a 1960s criticism of social convention and the restriction of desire to bourgeois or 'familial' forms. (There was a general movement of 'anti-psychiatry' that included the figures of R. D. Laing (1927–) and Wilhelm Reich (1897–1957), who are quoted throughout *Anti-Oedipus*.) Rather than *using* reason and reasoned arguments, the book sought to explain and historicise the emergence of an essentially repressive image of reason. Rather than argument and proposition it worked by questions and interrogation: why *should* we accept conventions, norms and values? What stops us from creating new values, new desires, or new images of what it is to be and think? This book was not a move within an already established debate; it shifted the entire criteria of debate. Against justification and legitimation, it put forward the power of creation and transformation. It did not adopt the single voice of universal reason but, like a novel, 'played' with the voices of those traditionally deemed to be at the margins of reason, such as women: 'The Women's Liberation movements are correct in saying: We are not castrated, so you get fucked' (Deleuze and Guattari 1983: 61).

In *Anti-Oedipus* Deleuze and Guattari create a whole new vocabulary and mode of composition. This was because, against conventional psychoanalysis, they challenged the idea that there was anything like a 'psyche' at all. There was no standard individual, person or self that could be the object of study or the aim of therapy. Rather, they created the term 'schizoanalysis' to describe their own approach and goal: not the primacy of the psyche but the primacy of parts, 'schizzes' or impersonal and mobile fragments. Instead of beginning from the assumption that there are fixed structures such as language or logic that order life – this would be a 'paranoid' fixation on some external order – they argued that life was an open and creative whole of proliferating connections. They celebrate the 'schizo' against paranoid 'man'. Their 'schizo' is not a psychological type (not a schizophrenic), but a way of thinking a life not governed by any fixed norm or image of self – a self in flux and becoming, rather than a self that has submitted to law. The schizo is a challenge to the way we think and write. Instead of accepting that we know what thinking is, and instead of seeing philosophy or psychoanalysis as the description of what the mind *is*, they argued that schizoanalysis would create new connections, open experience up to new beginnings, and allow us to think differently.

In addition to his creative response to structuralism and psycho-analysis Deleuze's work can also be seen as a radicalisation of phenom-enology. The German philosophers Edmund Husserl and Martin Heidegger had argued that we too readily accept the presuppositions of what human life is (such as man as a 'rational animal'). To *really think*, they insisted, would require looking at life as it appears in the flow of time and becoming, rather than determining life from some already determined fixed viewpoint (such as that of the knowing and judging 'subject'). We need to address the dynamic flux of experience as it becomes through time, and not as it is determined by pre-given and ready-made concepts. Phenomenology, therefore, was an attention to *phenomena* or appearances. Deleuze transformed and radicalised this renewal of what it is to think with his concept of the *simulacra*. Phenomena are appearances *of* some world, but *simulacra* are appear-ances in themselves, with no origin or foundation 'behind' them. Deleuze used the work of a vast range of philosophers, going back to Plato, but his general project of becoming and the 'simulacra' can be seen as a radical critique of phenomenology. Phenomenology had insisted that we need to look at the world in its fluctuating appearances, and not in terms of fixed concepts or logic. Deleuze's genius lay in taking this notion of appearances (images or 'simulacra') well beyond its conventional philosophical home. Deleuze insisted that if we *really* want to accept the appearance of the world without judgement or pre-supposition then we will not refer to appearances as appearances *of* some world; there will be nothing other than a 'swarm' of appearances – with no foundation of the experiencing mind or subject. Simulacra are appearances or images without ground or foundation. Deleuze looked at the way *all life*, not just human minds, creates and expresses itself through images. Even the smallest organism is an event of simulation, or the interaction of appearances. The cell that becomes through photo-synthesis does not 'perceive' light as an image *of* something. The relation between cell and light is just an interaction of appearances without any underlying or more 'real' ground. Deleuze even considered the in-human appearances and perceptions of machines and cameras. In fact, one of the most important events in Deleuze's thought was the advent of modern cinema, where images were freed from the human eye and from organising perspective and narrative. It is cinema's power to 'see' in an inhuman and multiple way that gives us, he argued, a whole new way of thinking.

This book therefore charts its way through Deleuze's criticism of conventional thinking and his invention of new styles of thought. To begin with we will look at how Deleuze defines philosophy, science and art. He gives strict definitions, not because he wants to impose one more system on thought, but because he wants to show that thinking takes *different* forms. Philosophy, science and art are distinct tendencies or powers, so it makes no sense to try to come up with some unified picture of the world – for there are as many worlds as there are ways of thinking or perceiving. Once we accept the distinct powers of thought, we can also look at the dynamic interaction of these powers. For Deleuze, we do not study philosophy or science to get to the truth of literature. We do not try to find the ideas or contexts that are then expressed in literary works, nor should we use literature as some form of document, example or evidence to support claims in history, philosophy or psychology.

The interaction of philosophy and art should create difference and divergence, rather than agreement and a common sense. Philosophy has to do with creating concepts, while art has to do with creating new experiences. But the two can transform each other. The creation of cinema challenged philosophers to rethink the relation between time and image; but new concepts in philosophy can also provoke artists into recreating the boundaries of experience. For this reason Deleuze drew upon all sorts of texts, insisting on their difference from each other *and* on their power to transform each other. His work does not provide a theory *of* literature so much as a way of forming questions through literature, questions that should challenge life. It is this challenging aspect of Deleuze's work, alongside his insistence to tear apart the very assumptions of common sense, that makes him both difficult and exciting to read. No introduction to Deleuze's work can be simple, for the ideas themselves are complex and confronting. The next chapter looks at how Deleuze defines the very relation between ideas and literature or art, before looking in the following chapter at how ideas can be transformed by new events in the arts such as cinema. The themes of becoming and difference will occur over and over again, and should become more precise as this book progresses. This ties in with Deleuze's concept of repetition. We need to *repeat* difference and thinking; the minute we feel we have grasped what thinking and difference *are* then we have lost the very power of difference. Repetition is not the re-occurrence of the same old thing over and over again; to repeat something is to begin again, to renew, to question, and to refuse remaining the same.

It would be 'unDeleuzean', then, to place Deleuze in his context, if by this we mean explaining how his ideas came about or how he reacted against certain dominant ideas. But this does not mean that we can't begin to think Deleuze *historically*. We just need a notion of history that is not one of unfolding development from a single human viewpoint. So we would have to see Deleuze's work as an active response to a host of problems from diverse areas, not just problems within philosophy. These included: the problem of capitalism and how we can think revolution; the problem of 'man' and how we can think evolution; the problem of thought and how we can think creation. History takes the form of co-existing lines, 'plateaus' or divergent series of becomings. This refers not just to the divergent time-lines of cultures, although Deleuze does describe primitive societies who have a time image of an eternal earth, while despotic societies regard the ruler as descended from a divine order. (And all these different cultural understandings of time overlap each other and co-exist.)

Deleuze also refers to the different 'speeds' of animal and plant life. Understanding what something *is* means understanding its duration, its power to perceive and contract the differences of its milieu. Human memory, for example, can perceive not just its own time and past, but a whole of time well beyond its actual perceptions. For Deleuze, we should take this power of memory, this power of the human, to become inhuman. We can think from the present or actual world to a virtual world or future that is not yet given. This book will explain and explore the way in which both philosophy and literature are distinct expressions of this power to become.

KEY IDEAS

1

POWERS OF THINKING

Philosophy, art and science

This chapter looks at how Deleuze defines philosophy in relation to art and science. For Deleuze it remains important to look at the specificity and difference of philosophy. This ties into his whole project of provoking and mobilising thinking. We should not see philosophy or art as disciplines or conventions – something that already is and that we can know and define; we need to see philosophy (or anything) in terms of its possibility or what it might be able to do. So we need to distinguish philosophy from art, for example, in order to avoid the homogenisation of thinking. We have a tendency today to assume that there is a common sense or agreed upon way of thinking, or that we should aim at such a common sense through communication and consensus. Against this, Deleuze wanted to open life up to diverse modes of thinking. Literature, for example, would not be based on representing or expressing some common world-view or shared experience; literature should shock, shatter and provoke experience. But there are different ways in which thought can be disrupted. To demonstrate this difference Deleuze made a distinction between philosophy, art and science.

The title of one of Deleuze's final works, co-authored with his long-time colleague the French psychoanalyst Félix Guattari, took the form of a question: *What is Philosophy?* (1994; published in French in 1991). It is in this late work that Deleuze and Guattari distinguish philosophy from art and science. But from the earliest point in his work Deleuze looked at philosophy as a *power*; not as a collection of texts, but as a permanent challenge to think differently by creating problems. While philosophy is a unique power it is also enabled by its encounter with other powers; events in science and art will require and provoke new problems in philosophy. Deleuze insisted that neither philosophy, nor art, nor science were 'academic' pursuits in search of disinterested knowledge. Rather, all thinking is an art and event of life and Deleuze regarded the three main modes of thinking – art, science and philosophy – as powers to transform life. According to Deleuze, we can define the distinction between literature, art and philosophy not by cataloguing literary and philosophical texts and finding some shared feature, but by looking at what they *do*, and what they do when they are extended and stretched to their utmost. Philosophy, art and science need to be seen as distinct moments of the explosive force of life, a life that is in a process of constant 'becoming'. It is not that we have a world or life that philosophers or writers then describe or interpret. Each act of art, science or philosophy is itself an event and transfiguration of life. And each transformation changes life in its own specific or singular way.

Reading a work *as* art or *as* philosophy requires that we see its specific force, or its capacity for rupturing life. We may never encounter a *pure* work of art or philosophy, but we can strive to distinguish and maximise artistic, philosophical and scientific tendencies within any text. We can distinguish these tendencies not by looking at what a work *is* but at what it achieves or does. Plato may have used literary metaphors but he did so in order to establish a philosophical truth above and beyond this world; scientists may use fictions or narratives, such as the 'big bang' but they do so in order to make the world we live in functional and manageable. Literature is the power of fiction itself: not making a claim about what the world *is*, but about the imagination of a possible world. Art is not about representation, concepts or judgement; art is the power to think in terms that are not so much cognitive and intellectual as *affective* (to do with feeling and sensible experience). We are not reading a work as artistic or literary if we read it for its representation of the world or its presentation of theories. Deleuze insisted that we *should* understand these distinctions, in order to push thought to each of its limits and to avoid bland notions of common sense. If we accept that thought takes one homogeneous form we fall into unquestioning opinion, reducing all science to 'stories' or all philosophy to fact-finding. We never really see what our thinking can do. If we *can* create philosophies, art and science then this tells us that thought is productive. If we understand the power that drives this production then we will be able to maximise our creativity, our life and our future.

Deleuze was a philosopher but he also wrote in a highly literary manner – using voices, characters and scenes worthy of science fiction. In *A Thousand Plateaus* (1987; published in French in 1980) Deleuze and Guattari construct a drama among competing theorists of natural science, drawn from different moments in history and overseen by a fictional character. Deleuze also wrote on literary authors and argued for the specific power of literature. If we want to understand what Deleuze has to offer *as a philosopher* we first have to understand the reason for philosophy in relation to literature and to science. Deleuze drew upon science and art, and presented some of his most challenging ideas in relation to cinema. His project, though, is ultimately philosophical, for he allowed the creations of literature and observations of science to make a repeated philosophical claim: a claim about the very force of life in general. Philosophy is just this power to create a general concept of life, giving form to the chaos of life. Any truly philosophical thought, therefore, will strive to think the whole of life: so it must encounter art and science but then go on to think the world beyond art and science. Science may give consistent descriptions of the *actual* world, such as the things we observe as 'facts' or 'states of affairs', but philosophy has the power to understand the virtual world. This is not the world as it is, but the world beyond any specific observation or experience: the very possibility of life. For Deleuze, the concept that best answers this power to think the whole of life is difference. Life is difference, the power to think differently, to become different and to create differences. The philosophical ability to think this concept will help us to live our lives in a more joyful and affirmative manner. Because philosophy allows the transformation of life, it is a power, not an academic discipline. Similarly, but in its own different way, art also encounters difference: not by producing a concept of difference but by presenting and creating differences (such as all the different characters in a novel or different sounds in a symphony). If we want to know what something (such as art, science or philosophy) *is*, then we can ask how it serves life. The problem, today, is that when we ask what art or philosophy are for we tend to feel they should serve some everyday function: making us better managers or communicators. We fail to see that the purpose or force of art and philosophy goes beyond what life *is* to what it might become. Today, no one really seems to ask what science is *for*, and this is probably because science is manifestly functional. Much of Deleuze's project was spent in showing a force of life beyond everyday function, such as the force and value of change and becoming: not a becoming *for* some preconceived end, but a becoming for the sake of change itself. Deleuze drew from science in all its forms, but he did so in order to extend the powers of literature and philosophy, all the while arguing for the necessity of literature and philosophy for life.

Deleuze's books on literary authors and his own uses of literature were then acts of philosophy, but for Deleuze philosophy and literature both required each other. Philosophy is not just something philosophers do, nor is it confined to those times when we are 'doing philosophy'. Philosophy is a tendency of all thinking. Common sense and everyday banal generalisations are just bad philosophy, for in appealing to common sense we have already formed a general concept of what it means to think. Deleuze begins by showing that we *already* work with an image of thought or some abstract notion of life: such as the image of common sense or the concept of life as matter. From this already given tendency for thinking of life in homogenising general terms, Deleuze asks that we do philosophy more explicitly and more adventurously. If we were to ask the question, 'Why Philosophy?, Deleuze would not say that it will make us clever, or solve problems or tidy up logical errors in our arguments. We do philosophy, not because it will clean up other areas of our lives, but because it is a dimension of life in its own right. We do philosophy because we *can*, and if we *can* do philosophy – if we can ask 'big' and possibly unsolvable questions – then we *ought* to. Why? For Deleuze life in general proceeds by creatively maximising its potential; philosophy is one of the directions by which a certain line of life (thinking) increases its power. For Deleuze there is a direct link between philosophy, literature and ethics. If we *limit* thought to simple acts of representation and cognition – 'this is a chair', 'this is a table' – then we impose all sorts of dogmas and rules upon thinking (Deleuze 1994: 135). We fail to extend life to its maximum. We use a creation of thought – logic and grammar – to imprison thought. The fact is that there are all sorts of texts and styles of thinking that go well beyond representation or simple pictures of the world. Not only philosophy but literature, art, cinema, stupidity, madness and malevolence all testify to a thinking that is not that of representation so much as production, mutation and creation. We do philosophy, then, not to conform to or correct some dogma of common sense; we do philosophy to expand thought to its infinite potential. In general, Deleuze insisted on the *universal* power of philosophy. This is not a power of *generalisation* or looking at some common feature that all beings share. Thinking universally demands that we go beyond all the beings that we perceive and think how any being might be possible. In *What is Philosophy?* Deleuze, with Guattari, defines this universalising power of philosophy more specifically as the power to create concepts. Deleuze had always intertwined references to science, art and philosophy, but in *What is Philosophy?* he and Guattari offer explicit accounts of philosophy as the creation of concepts, art as the creation of percepts and affects and science as the creation of functions.

CONCEPTS

Both literature and philosophy carry thought beyond common sense and representation in different but connected ways. Philosophy, according to Deleuze, creates concepts. Concepts are not labels or names that we attach to things; they produce an orientation or a direction for thinking. A concept in this philosophical sense is quite different from an everyday concept. At a day-to-day level, for example, we might use the concept of happiness. 'Happy Birthday', 'Andrew and Elizabeth are a happy couple', 'Do whatever makes you happy', 'Seven steps to happiness'. Day-to-day usage of concepts works like shorthand or habit; we use concepts so that we *do not* have to think. We say, 'Happy Birthday', not because we want to *say* or mean something, but because that is just what we do. Everyday concepts, then, allow life to carry on in an orderly or functional manner. But here, as elsewhere, Deleuze refuses to see the everyday or common form of something as the essence of something. Our day-to-day concepts do not capture what a concept is because they do not allow the full force of what a concept can do. Indeed, for Deleuze, if we want to understand what thinking is we should not gather examples from everyday life and draw conclusions; we should look at thinking in its most extreme forms (such as art, philosophy, stupidity, madness or ill will). The philosophical concept bears little relation to the concepts of everyday language, just as Deleuze's definitions of art and cinema will seem to be at odds with our common viewing experiences. One overwhelming reason for reading Deleuze lies in this rather unfashionable 'high-culture' affirmation of art and philosophy as distinct from ordinary life and popular culture. For Deleuze, our daily use of concepts follows the model of representation and opinion, where we assume that there's a present world that we then re-present in concepts, and that we all aim for agreement, communication and information. A philosophical use of concepts does not follow opinion and everyday usage. It is creative rather than representational and this has a direct bearing on life and literature.

Opinion, for Deleuze, is the very inertia or failure of thinking. Opinion is a laziness directly opposed to the expansiveness of the philosophical concept. Deleuze and Guattari cite the example of a man who moves from his dislike for a certain type of cheese to a general claim that the cheese just *is* offensive (Deleuze and Guattari 1994: 146). It is this tendency of opinion to reduce the difference of the world to being 'just like me' that both weakens the active character of thought *and* reinforces the modern capitalist prejudice that we are 'all the same' and capable of interacting in one global market:

> In every conversation the fate of philosophy is always at stake, and many philosophical discussions do not as such go beyond discussions of cheese, including the insults and the confrontation of worldviews. The philosophy of communication is exhausted in the search for a universal liberal opinion as consensus, in which we find again the cynical perceptions and affections of the capitalist himself.
>
> (Deleuze and Guattari 1994: 146)

In opinion, then, we move from a particular experience and use it to form some whole that *reduces* difference and complexity. Everyday opinions are bland and reductive generalisations. I am annoyed by the asylum seeker who lives next door, therefore all asylum seekers are lazy. I am not turned on by meaningless same-sex encounters, therefore all extra-marital relations are evil. Opinion moves from my specific likes and desires and homogenises desire, producing a general 'subject'. A philosophical concept work against this reductive and generalising tendency by expanding difference. It creates new ways of thinking. Take the concept of love. Opinion will reduce love to its already known forms – bourgeois marriage – and then dismiss all other forms: 'That's not love; it's perversion!' A concept in its philosophical sense moves beyond any example or model to think the very power or possibility: so 'love' would not be reducible to any given form, whether that be familial, homosexual or heterosexual. We might form a concept of love, as Deleuze did, that was as open as possible (Deleuze 1973: 140). Love is the encounter with another person that opens us up to a possible world. This concept does not take a form of love – the couple – and then say that this is what love *is*. The *concept* of love as 'a possible encounter with an other as a whole new world' allows us to think of forms of love that are not yet given, that are not actual but virtual. A concept, for Deleuze, is just this power to move beyond what we know and experience to think how experience might be extended.

A concept does not just add another word to a language; it transforms the whole shape of a language. We can get a sense of this by going back to the concept of 'happiness'. One of the philosophers most frequently cited by Deleuze, Friedrich Nietzsche (1844–1900), created a number of concepts that were crucial for Deleuze's project. The first thing to note about a philosophical concept is that it cannot be looked at in isolation. If I ask you for a definition of 'happiness' you might say, 'what makes you feel good', or 'what we're all aiming for'. But philosophical concepts cannot have these succinct definitions because they create a whole new path for thinking: the concept of happiness would not refer to this or that instance of happiness; it would have to *enact or create* a new possibility or thought of happiness. Philosophical concepts are not amenable to dictionary style definitions, for their power lies in being open and expansive. For this reason we have to understand them through the new connections that they make. Nietzsche, for example, used a number of interrelated concepts to challenge the idea that thinking was a picture of representation of the world. Thinking and concepts, he argued, take the flux of reality and cut it up into manageable units. All thinking for Nietzsche was a type of metaphor – substituting a fixed image for a fluid reality – and we can never be literal or say exactly what we see. Take the word 'leaf'. We might think that it originally refers to the green growths on a tree, and that we then use the word metaphorically to refer to a 'leaf' of paper. The problem is, of course, that the word 'leaf' is just as arbitrary whether it is used to refer to trees or books. In both cases we have to take the infinitely different – each different and varying leaf – and fix some word that will apply to all leaves. This gives us the illusion that there is some general type – say, 'leafness' – to which language refers. We imagine that there are fixed forms which our language labels or which can be pointed to, *literally and concretely*, in language. Against this, Nietzsche insists that language *creates* concepts; all language, not just literary language, is metaphorical. It takes the concrete and sensible world and refers to it through something else, such as the sign or the concept. All language, then, *by virtue of the fact that it is language*, is creative. We have, however, developed the illusion that there *is* some truth behind language, and we imagine that there are some ways of speaking or writing (such as science) that will get us out of metaphor and give us the 'true' world. But there is no 'true' world behind appearances, only further appearances. There is no essential 'truth' above and beyond the sensible flux of life. Once something appears to us we have already organised it into a certain perspective, and life would not be able to continue if we did not perceive the world in our own interested but necessarily partial way. This is not a distortion of the true world; this is just what the world is: appearances with no higher truth. We have, according to Nietzsche, fallen into despair precisely because we have constructed this notion of the 'true' world beyond language and appearances. When we cannot reach this world we collapse into *nihilism*.

According to Deleuze, Nietzsche was the first thinker to conceive of the world in terms of 'pre-personal singularities' (Deleuze 1990: 102): that is, not general forms that language can organise, but chaotic and free-roaming fluxes. So concepts do not label or systematise reality, for reality in itself has no order or fixed being; concepts *create* this order. So philosophical concepts, for both Deleuze and Nietzsche, ought to be *active*. They should present themselves as creations, not as representations. Nietzsche's concepts were, for this reason, resistant to simple definition or demonstration, for they were *not* meant to look like simple labels. They were *active* – explicitly creating connections – rather than *reactive* – presenting themselves as simple labels of a world already ordered. (Deleuze makes much of the ethics of active and reactive in his book on Nietzsche, published in French in 1962, as part of a wave of new and radical readings of Nietzsche [Deleuze

NIHILISM

According to Nietzsche, nihilism is the logical end-point of Western philosophy. Philosophy begins with a life project of asceticism: renouncing desires for the sake of some higher or better world (such as the world of truth). We imagine a truer and better world beyond appearances. When we fail to grasp that true world we fall into despair or nihilism, for we have lost that higher world that we never had. The consequence is *ressentiment*. We still feel the loss of some higher or better world, and so we imagine ourselves to be guilty, punished or outcast. This reaches its pitch in Christianity where we are permanently guilty in an irredeemably fallen world. For Nietzsche, the proper response to this fall into nihilism, decadence and ressentiment is not to find another basis of truth but to abandon our enslavement to truth. We need to have the force and courage to live with this world here and now.

1983].) Concepts are not correct pictures of the world; we should not be striving to create a science or theory that is as close to the world as possible. Concepts are philosophical precisely because they create possibilities for thinking beyond what is already known or assumed. Nietzsche's concept of happiness is a case in point. Whereas everyday concepts point to some external meaning – such that we can ask, 'what *is* happiness?' – Nietzsche's concepts strive to create multiple and diverse effects. 'Happiness' or a 'joyous science', according to Nietzsche (1882), would free itself of the illusion of some ultimate true world or some privileged knowledge. Happiness is the capacity or power to live one's life *actively* – affirming the particularity or specificity of one's moment in time. We live *reactively*, by contrast, if we try to find some true world above and beyond the world that appears to us. Nietzsche's concept of 'happiness' is not just different from everyday understanding; in forming this concept Nietzsche had to create a series of concepts and a new mode or style of thinking.

We ought to be able to see from the complexity of just one of Nietzsche's concepts that such terms cannot be summed up with a definition; we cannot understand 'happiness' in Nietzsche without changing our basic assumptions. A concept (in this radical sense) does not just add one more word to our vocabulary; it renders many of our present terms incoherent. How, for example, can we say that there is no 'truth'? Can we say that it is true that there is no truth? Wouldn't this just present itself as another truth? A concept provokes us, dislodges us from our ways of thinking and opens experience up to new 'intensities': a way of seeing differently. Nietzsche does not just add the concept of 'happiness' to language; the concept changes how language works (Nietzsche 1961). For Deleuze philosophy is just this capacity to create concepts that re-orient our thinking. And this leads us to the importance of philosophy for literature, and the importance of literature in its own right. A concept is not a word; it is the creation of a way of thinking. Deleuze therefore has a quite specific understanding of language that goes against the grain of everyday opinion and a lot of recent literary theory. For Deleuze, language is not just a system of signs or conventions that we impose upon the world in order to organise or differentiate our experience. Any actual language or system of signs – say, modern English – is only possible because of a prior *problem*. The formation of a language responds to a way of approaching the world, so that language is an action, or a constant question and creation in response to experience. So *words* are dependent upon tasks or paths (differentiations) through which we approach what is other than ourselves; a word gives order to a sense which pre-exists it.

We can only have the modern word 'sexuality', for example, because we assume that each person has a certain sexual identity or orientation that we can refer to. And this idea is only possible because we have the modern idea of unique individuals who, above and beyond their actions and bodies, also have an inner self or subjectivity. These concepts – of sexuality, the self, identity – are themselves only possible because of the specific *problems* that characterise and create us. Perhaps, today, we are oriented by the problems: 'who am I?' or 'what is a self?' It is because our lives move within the *sense* of these questions that we can articulate concepts like 'sexuality' that refer back to the problem of the personal. Language is more than a set of *actual* words; it is also the *virtual* dimension of sense, or the problems that our words organise and articulate. Because language is always more than its actual elements, we can have the same concept or sense, but in different languages. The *actual* words 'happiness' or 'bonheur' are different but evoke the same sense or meaning. Sense is virtual and is activated whenever such words are used, meant or thought. (A book is an actual set of pages and marks, but its sense is virtual.) Philosophical concepts create new problems and new milieus of sense.

Language – the system of different words – is for Deleuze the actualisation of far more profound differences. The words of our language try to give some consistency to the chaotic and infinite differences of experience and life. Words and other cultural phenomena are ways of managing difference, but we can also use words to refine and enhance difference. Concepts, for example, can take a simple word, such as the everyday word 'happiness' which we use to cover a variety of different cases, and then rethink this word (as Nietzsche did) in a far more nuanced way. The words of our language, or the actual system of differences, are possible only because we have already oriented ourselves in some way in a milieu of sense. We can have the word 'happiness' only because we think about certain distinctions, and it is always possible to give this word new sense by re-thinking distinctions. Deleuze would not say, therefore, that we think a certain way because we speak English; nor would he allow that language 'constructs' our world or reality. On the contrary, we need to look beyond the actual terms of our language to the questions and problems it presupposes. Problems, here, are not like quiz-show questions where there are right answers just waiting to be revealed. A problem is a way of creating a future. When plants grow and evolve they do so by way of problems, developing features to avoid predators, to maximise light or to retain moisture. And the problem of 'light' is posed, creatively, by different forms of life in different ways: photosynthesis for plants, the eye for animal organisms, colour for the artist. A problem is life's way of responding to or questioning what is not itself. When a philosopher poses a problem this allows her to produce new concepts. Nietzsche created the concepts of 'happiness', 'joy' and 'innocence' in response to the problem of nihilism: why are we enslaved to the idea of a true world beyond language and appearances? Deleuze created a vast number of concepts. His concept of 'singularities', for example, tried to think all those differences which we fail to notice, recognise or conceptualise. He therefore works against the tendency for thought to settle with what is most obvious or least resistant.

AFFECT

If philosophy takes language away from simple definitions and the fixity of opinions to concepts and problems, art creates affects and percepts. Affections are what happens to us (disgust, or the recoil of the nostrils at the smell of cheese); perceptions are what we receive (odour, or the smell itself). Affects and percepts, in art, free these forces from the particular observers or bodies who experience them. At its simplest level imagine the presentation of 'fear' in a novel, even though it is not we who are afraid. Affects are sensible experiences in their *singularity*, liberated from organising systems of representation. A poem might create the affect of fear without an object feared, a reason, or a person who is afraid. Many of the poems of Emily Dickinson (1830–86) describe the most harmless objects and situations but do so through a language and mood of terror. Part of this is achieved not so much by referring to objects but through rhythms and pauses, so that it is the sense of absence, of halting, of hesitation or holding back that creates an affect of fear: a fear that is not located in a character nor directed to an object. Poem 287, below, uses the typical Dickinson technique of images separated by dashes, such that it is the object and its linked affects rather than any speaker or character at the heart of the poem. The poem takes the point of view of an object, a stopped clock.

> A Clock stopped –
> Not the Mantel's –
> Geneva's farthest skill
> Can't put the puppet bowing –
> That just now dangled still –
>
> An awe came on the Trinket!
> The Figures hunched, with pain –
> Then quivered out the Decimals –
> Into Degreeless Noon –
>
> It will not stir for Doctors –
> This Pendulum of snow –
> This Shopman importunes it –
> While cool – concernless, No –
>
> Nods from the Gilded pointers –
> Nods from the Seconds slim –
> Decades of Arrogance between
> The Dial life –
> And Him –
>
>   (Dickinson 1975)

The clock presents time stopped, an impersonal death or absence of life. The feeling mentioned in the poem is detached from any person, 'An awe . . .'. This poem presents the concrete image of a broken machine. The affect of fear is created through the disjunction between the obstinately broken and stubborn clock that resists all repair and the time that marches on and breaks all life in an impersonal 'Arrogance'. Even though the poem makes some gesture to the God that inscrutably withdraws all life in time ('And Him'), this is not a recognisable God who will help us locate and delimit fear. Fear, terror, absence and separation are not named *in* the poem but are evoked between the images we have of time ('The Dial Life') and the ultimate command of time ('And Him . . .'). Dickinson's poems take the affect of fear away from everyday recognition – where we fear what threatens us personally, such as earthquakes and other disasters – to a 'fear' that is presented impersonally.

The twentieth-century English playwright, Harold Pinter (1930 –), was a great creator of the affect of 'boredom'. This is achieved by long pauses in the dialogue, by characters who exchange questions (rather than questions and answers), by interactions that seem to have no reference or direction. It is not his characters who are bored, nor are his plays boring; but they convey the boredom of modern bourgeois life. Boredom is created as a general affect. We are presented with 'boredom' – not bored persons or a boring play. It is this creation of impersonal affects that enables art to dissect the order of everyday experience. In day-to-day life we find ourselves simply rejecting a novel or person because they are 'boring'; we act as though boredom were a simple object that we can identify. But great art disengages affects such that we are no longer capable of simply identifying and delimiting the feelings of boredom, or fear or desire. It is the task of art to dislodge affects from their recognised and expected origins. Pinter's plays are presentations of affect precisely in those milieus where they are least expected: such as the menace or terror of marriages and bourgeois life (*The Lover*) or the hostility and violence of acts of charity and hospitality (*The Caretaker*).

Affect, as presented in art, disrupts the everyday and opinionated links we make between words and experience. We have already seen the way in which, for Deleuze, everyday opinions generalise and reduce concepts to their already known forms. Everyday opinion is also limiting, Deleuze argues, because it assumes that there simply *is* a common world, there to be shared through language as information and communication. Opinion not only assumes a present and shared world; it also assumes a common sense whereby thinking takes the same 'upright' form distributed among rational perceivers. *Opinion* or *doxa* makes a direct link between affect and concept, between what we see and what we say, or between the sensible and the intelligible. Opinion speaks as though the world were easily translatable into a common language and experience that we all share. To return to our cheese example, imagine that someone brings some gorgonzola to the dinner table and the smell assaults my nostrils (as affect). I do not just say, 'I don't like this'. I say, 'That's not food', or 'No one with any taste could consume that'. I pass directly from a sensible affect – my body recoiling at the odour – to a concept – the 'badness' of this cheese. In opinion we pass all too easily between affects on the one hand and concepts on the other. It is as though we have already determined the limits and locations of, say, fear or boredom (to return to Dickinson and Pinter). But art can open us up to whole new possibilities of affect: seeing terror from the image of a clock, or a boredom that pervades life in general. For the purposes of life everyday thinking has to work by a kind of shorthand. From a highly complex flow of perceptions I tend to perceive recognisable and repeatable objects. I do not perceive all the minute differences that make up the flow of time. I see this as an extended object that *is* the same. I regard myself, not as a flow of perceptions, but as a person with an identity. So, when I experience data – such as colour, sound or texture – I subordinate it to an everyday concept. Art works in the other direction. It disengages the ordered flow of experience into its singularities. We will look at how this works in literary art in the chapter on minor literature. In the chapter that follows, we will consider the case of a visual art, such as cinema. Each art form, Deleuze insisted, also has its own specific power.

Just as we cannot assume that there simply *is* a unified thinking subject who is the same whether he is doing philosophy, art or science, neither can we assume that all the forms of art can be traced back to some common ground. What we *can* acknowledge is that art is not about knowledge, conveying 'meanings' or providing information. Art is not just an ornament or style used to make data more palatable or consumable. Art may well have meanings or messages but what makes it *art* is not its content but its *affect*, the sensible force or style through which it produces content. Why, for example, would we spend two hours in the cinema watching a film if all we wanted were the story or the moral message? However much it is mixed with other functions the fact that we do produce styles and sensible affects in art discloses something about what our thinking can do – that minds are not just machines for information or communication but that we also desire and work with affect.

PROBLEMS, CREATION AND ETHICS

Deleuze is true to his insistence that concepts are responses to problems. His concepts of philosophy and literature responded to a particular problem: why does thinking limit itself to banal and puerile cases? Deleuze creates a specific concept of literature. Literature does not refer to books or literary studies; it allows us to think of a way of stretching language to its limits. Deleuze's created concept of philosophy refers to a capacity to think differently. Deleuze therefore creates a *concept* of philosophy that rejuvenates what we usually understand by the *word* philosophy. So the concept of 'philosophy' for Deleuze allows us to think against the normal or recognised cases of thinking. Philosophy usually begins with thoroughly unremarkable instances of everyday life that presuppose an already given and unchanging image of thought: 'This is a chair' and so on (Deleuze 1994: 135). Deleuze's new concept of philosophy as the creation of concepts strives to take thought beyond normality and recognition. How can we free thought from these restricting images?

To begin with we need to create new concepts (through philosophy) and new percepts and affects (through art). Affects and percepts, which are the outcome of art, are possibilities that Deleuze wants to think of *impersonally*. Just as a mile is a scientific function because it measures space impersonally – we do not think of a mile as 12 minutes walk but as what is uniform whether traversed by foot, cycle or car – so an affect or percept approaches sensibility impersonally. Henry James's novel *The Wings of the Dove* presents 'desire' as an impersonal affect; it presents not just the desire of this or that character but provokes or evokes a general *sense* of desire. A horror film presents horror; for beyond the fear of the characters or the viewer there is just a *sense* of horror which the film draws upon. The film is not about horror, or a representation of horror; it is a sense or feeling of horror which we may or may not enter. Before the viewer or a character is actually horrified we view within the affect or milieu of horror in general. Just as art creates impersonal affects and percepts and science creates impersonal functions — say, by thinking of time and space in measurements which do not rely on any specific observer — so philosophy creates impersonal concepts. The concept is an impersonal creation precisely because it is not the expression of what 'I think'; it is an attempt to create thought beyond any already given 'I' or 'subject'. But we will only be able to truly create philosophically and artistically if we have an expansive concept of what creation is.

For Deleuze, creation is not an act of variation added on to an otherwise stable and inert life; it is not as though there is life and *then* the event or act of creation. All life is creation but according to its specific or 'singular' tendencies. We understand what something is not by looking to its unchanging form but by trying to discern its specific way of being different or creating, its specific problem. So, if we want to understand the problem that motivated Deleuze we need to look at the concepts of art and philosophy that he created. Creating these concepts, he felt, would open us up to new powers of thinking. Not only did this creativity not reside in philosophy alone, it is also important to recognise the difference between the creations of philosophy and literature. If we think that there *is* some ultimate truth or meaning, then it would not matter how we approach or represent it. It would not matter whether we use philosophy to give us the logic of the world, science to give a lawful account of the world, or art to represent the world. (All three would supposedly converge on the same world, there to be represented.) But, as we have seen, Deleuze insists that the world is not something outside thinking that is simply there waiting to be represented. We cannot separate thought from life, or the act of thinking the world from the world itself. Like any other mode of life, thought creates its own 'worlds'. Deleuze makes a distinction between the worlds we live and the 'cosmos', which is articulated through these worlds. There is no single world, which is then variously represented by science, art or philosophy. There is the world of science: of functions, laws and 'states of affairs'. Philosophy creates a world or 'plane' of concepts'; art creates a world of affects and percepts.

We have seen that for Deleuze, opinion creates a generalised 'subject' and assumes a common world, moving directly from affect to concept. Deleuze and Guattari argue that the very existence of opinion is political: 'It abstracts an abstract quality from perception and a general power from affection: in this sense all opinion is already political' (Deleuze and Guattari 1994: 145). Is this not just the way our fixed moral judgements and prejudices operate? I hear an Asian dialect on the bus that I do not understand and I say, 'That's not a civilised language'. Someone practises a form of sexuality that is not to my liking and I say, 'That's perverse', or 'That's evil'. Over and over again Deleuze insisted that he was working towards an ethics that was 'beyond good and evil'. This would mean that instead of assuming that there are values or meanings (good and evil) attached to the world, such that we can pass from the world to judgement without question, we need to look at how we pass from the world we perceive in our own specific, sensible and singular way, to concepts, judgements and values. To this end we need to separate affect and concept.

Recall that for Deleuze concepts are not just labels that we attach to things. Philosophy displays concepts as creations, productive of the way we approach and perceive things. Art, by contrast, concerns itself with affects and percepts. We destroy opinion and common sense by pulling our thinking apart. We ought not assume that there is a simple order to the world, where values are there to be found. We need to look at how we compose our perceptions of the world, the force of those perceptions (affect) and how we create decisions, judgements and concepts.

SUMMARY

Deleuze describes three powers of thinking, which are expressed in science, art and philosophy. Science fixes the world into observable 'states of affairs'. Philosophy creates concepts; these concepts do not label or represent the world so much as produce a new way of thinking and responding to problems. Art creates affects and percepts. Affections and perceptions are located within a specific person or point of view; but the affect and percept is a feeling or image freed from interested or organising subjects. The three powers have a discordant or divergent relation to each other. We cannot add up all we know from philosophy and science, and all we have felt through art, to come up with some coherent picture of *the* world. On the contrary, if we express the true power of each tendency in thinking we will realise the very differences of the worlds we live.

2

CINEMA

Perception, time and becoming

In this chapter we will be looking at Deleuze's two books on cinema, published in French in 1983 and 1985: *Cinema 1: The Movement-Image* and *Cinema 2: The Time-Image*. On the one hand, these books are clearly *about* cinema, for Deleuze was always striving to see the specificity of each mode of art and human thought. He did not see cinema as just another way of presenting stories and information; the very mode of cinematic form altered the possibilities for thinking and imagining. On the other hand, these are also works of philosophy. Not only does Deleuze draw on the French philosopher Henri Bergson (1859–1941), he uses cinema to theorise time, movement and life as a whole. But there is a clear reason why Deleuze combines an analysis of cinema with his most general philosophical claims. Deleuze argues that philosophy must remain open to life. Cinema is perhaps, as we will see here, one of the most important events of modern life. Only with cinema can we think of a mode of 'seeing' that is not attached to the human eye. Cinema, then, offers something like a 'percept': a reception of data that is not located in a subject. But Deleuze takes the possibility of cinema even further. Confronting cinema will open us up to a new philosophy, and it will do so not because we *apply* philosophy to films, but because we allow the creation of films to transform philosophy. Deleuze approaches cinema by way of two broad concepts: the movement-image of early cinema and the time-image of modern cinema. This then allows a reconsideration of time and movement, and so we are once again in the domain of the problem of life as a whole. Both of Deleuze's books on cinema express some of his most crucial arguments regarding the capacity of life to go beyond its human, recognisable and already given forms. This is mainly achieved through the imagination of time, and it is cinema, according to Deleuze, that offers an image of time itself.

Deleuze wrote two books on cinema in which he used the radical possibilities of cinema to explore some of his most important concepts, including the virtual, the time-image and the 'percept'. Indeed, the concept of the 'time-image', which is provoked by cinema, also enables us to rethink the very nature of concepts. For the time-image is, according to Deleuze, a presentation of time itself, which forces us to confront the very becoming and dynamism of life. But while Deleuze used cinema as an instance of the way in which an art-form could transform thought, cinema was always more than an 'example'. To deal with the specificity of cinema, he argued, we might also have to re-think philosophy: 'Cinema itself is a new practice of images and signs, whose theory philosophy must produce as conceptual practice' (Deleuze 1989, 280). In what follows we will be looking at the way cinema demands a whole new style of thinking, such that its ramifications can be gauged well beyond cinema. Deleuze traces the power of cinema in the transition from the movement-image to the time-image. The movement-image is the first shock of cinema, where the play of camera angles moving across a visual field gives us the direct expression of movement, and thereby opens thought up to the very mobility of life. In the time-image we are no longer presented with time indirectly – where time is what connects one movement to another – for in the time-image we are presented with *time itself*. There is a key point of methodology here. We begin understanding by looking at whatever it is we are trying to understand in its utmost specificity, so we look at cinema in its own terms and not just as another mode of art. But once we understand the specificity and difference of this one thing it will allow us to re-think any other thing, for the whole of life is transformed by each minute difference.

method

THE CINEMATIC

Cinematic affect is unique to cinema, so we should not treat film as a secondary form of literature. The person who complains that the film is 'nothing like the book' ought to read the book. (Similarly, the scientist who complained about a philosophy being 'inaccurate' or a philosopher who complained about a novel being 'illogical' would merely be imposing their own dogmatic image of thought on thought's other possibilities.) Cinematic affect is best revealed when cinema is at its most cinematic, when it is not trying to copy everyday vision or recreate a novel in a literary manner, by beginning with a voice-over narration of the first paragraph, for example. In order to understand what is cinematic about cinema we need to ask how cinema works. It takes a number of images and connects them to form a sequence, and it cuts and connects sequences using the inhuman eye of the camera, which can therefore create a number of competing viewpoints or angles. What makes cinema *cinematic* is this liberation of the sequencing of images from any single observer, so the affect of cinema is the presentation of an 'any point whatever'. Our everyday seeing of the world is always a *seeing from* our interested and *embodied* perspective. I organise the flow of perceptions into 'my' world. I see this *as* a chair or *as* a table, and I can do so only because I presuppose a world (my world) in which there is furniture and all the organising schemas this rests upon (a world of work, offices and so on). Cinema, however, can present images or perception liberated from this organising structure of everyday life and it does this by maximising its own internal power. The maximisation of an internal power is the opposite of convergence. If cinema were trying to rewrite nineteenth-century novels or become the faithful medium of science and documentary, then it would be striving to overcome what marks it out as cinema. If, however, cinema were to maximise its own power – by intensifying its connection, cutting and sequencing of images – then it would be diverging from other modes of thought. In so doing – in becoming infinitely cinematic – cinema can offer a challenge to the whole of life. The very techniques cinema uses to follow life – image sequences – can also be used to transform life, by disrupting sequences. Deleuze will explain how the technique of cinema that begins with a realism that strives to represent life eventually develops to alter the possible perception of life.

Cinema, like everyday perception, connects a flow of different images into ordered wholes. However, there are also moments of cinema where by extending this very process cinema takes us away from actualised objects and wholes to the very flow of images. Instead of connecting or synthesising images into *meaningful* progressions, cinema can present images in their 'purely optical' form (Deleuze 1989: 2). In the film *Traffic* by Steven Soderbergh (2001), for example, the story oscillates between clear and 'realisitic' sequences of middle-class America and sepia-toned images of Mexico. The yellowish colour of the Mexican 'story' precludes us from viewing the whole as a single and coherent narrative. It is as if the 'Mexican' or 'other' tale were clearly presented *as* image, *as* viewed, *as* a projection of the American cinema's imagination. The film itself, the material of film – its yellow-ness – is not something we see through to grasp reality; we see 'seeing'. For Deleuze cinema has this power of releasing us from our tendency to organise images into some shared external world. We see imaging itself. Or, more accurately, there is no organising and presupposed 'we' so much as a presentation of 'imaging'.

If we could perceive without imposing our interested or practical connections and selection on to images then we might get a sense of the image itself. Art, in general, is just this capacity to present what Deleuze refers to as 'affects' and 'percepts'. More specifically, Deleuze argues, the art of cinema is not just its freedom from conceptual organ-isation and interested viewpoint, but its images of time and movement. What makes the machine-like movement of the cinema so important is that the camera can 'see' or 'perceive' without imposing concepts. The camera does not organise images from a fixed point but itself moves across movements. This is the power of the movement-image, which we will look at in more detail below: the power to free move-ment from an organising viewpoint. Similarly, our standard perception of time is also located and interested, with the past being those images I recall in order to live my future. Furthermore, we tend to think time *from* movement; from our fixed point of observation we use time to chart the changes around us. Time, conventionally, is thought of or represented as a 'now' or 'present' which connects the various moments of movement into a perceived whole. For this reason we tend to spatialise time, seeing time as a line connecting the various points of an action.

The power of cinema, for Deleuze, lies in its ability to give us direct and indirect images of time itself, not a time derived from movement. We get an indirect image of time from the *movement-image*: if the camera itself moves while the moving body also moves, and then the camera creates another movement across another moving body,

linear time (margin annotation)

we no longer think of movement as the synthesis of points within a single line of time. We see movement itself, in all its diversity, *from which* single points of view are composed. In the *time-image*, which is far more complex, we get a direct image of time. Think of time as the power of difference or becoming whereby we move from the virtual to the actual, from all the possible creations and tendencies to actualised events. For Deleuze this means that the time we experience is split in two. There is the past or impersonal memory which is virtual and the actual lines of lived time. The world or life we live is an actualisation of this pure or impersonal memory, but memory or time in its pure and whole state can also interrupt our world. In literature, for example, Deleuze writes that a character's day-to-day connected experiences can be disrupted by an event from the past, such as a singular childhood memory. Think of James Joyce's *A Portrait of the Artist as a Young Man* (1964 [1916]) where Stephen Dedalus does not just speak English but recalls a time when the words appeared to him as noise or sound, not yet meaningful or habitual. A memory can interrupt the actual present only because memory is real and exists virtually alongside the present. From such a personal memory, such as Stephen recalling the very beginnings of language, we can pass to *impersonal memory*: the idea of the language as belonging to no actual speaker, as the past of 'us' all, as the past from which we emerge. This interruption of the sequence of time by the virtual gives us a new image of time, a time that moves forward in day-to-day action, connecting images for the sake of life, *and* a time of memory that holds all the events and becomings of life in a whole. Time moves forward, producing actual worlds in ordered sequences, but time also has an eternal and virtual element, including all the tendencies opening towards the future and a past that can always intervene. In cinema of a certain style we get an image of this virtual–actual split and this is done by 'irrational cuts'. We are presented with sounds that do not coincide with visual images. The visual images are composed and ordered, not to form moving things or ordered wholes, but images as such – not images *of* some world from some point of view. This yields *singularities*: for example, a sense of movement that is not the movement *of* this body *from* this point of view. Singularities are the impersonal events from which we compose the world into actual bodies. A cinema of singularities would present colours, movements, sounds, textures, tones and lights that are not connected and organised into recognised and ordered wholes. In so doing it would take us back from the ordered world we view at a day-to-day level and allow us to think the singular and specific differences from which life is lived:

> Singularities are the true transcendental events. . . . Far from being individual or personal, singularities preside over the genesis of individuals and persons; they are distinguished in a 'potential' which admits neither Self nor I, but which produces them by actualizing or realizing itself. . . . Only a theory of the singular point is capable of transcending the synthesis of the person and the analysis of the individual as these are (or are made) in consciousness. . . . Only when the world, teeming with anonymous and nomadic, impersonal and preindividual singularities, opens up, do we tread at last on the field of the transcendental.
>
> (Deleuze 1990: 103)

CINEMA, THE UNIVERSAL AND THE ETHICS OF THINKING

When we view cinema we do, though, tend to interpret or synthesise the data into narratives, characters and meanings. Just because the most common forms of cinema or the majority of films work in a thoroughly unremarkable way does not mean that we should accept this as all that cinema is capable of. On the contrary, Deleuze's definitions of anything – thought, perception, cinema, science, the novel – claim to explain not what something *is* but its genesis, or how it becomes. This means looking at something carried to its 'nth power'. What do madness, stupidity and malevolence tell us about thinking? What do viral and genetic mutations, rather than fixed species, tell us about life? Science, for example, is not the collection or totality of scientific statements; it is a capacity to view the world in terms of states of affairs by impartial observers. We define something by its style of becoming and not by its already given forms. What would cinema be if we pushed it to the limit? Cinema is produced not from synthesised wholes and human observers but from the machinic and singular images of cameras, using cuts and multiple viewpoints.

Like all art, then, it is possible for cinema to *work* in such a way that its process of becoming – the disconnection or singularity of its images – is displayed. Affect, in general, is just a sensible or sensibility *not* organised into meaning. (Affect is in some ways the opposite of a concept. A concept allows us to think a form or connection without sensibility; we can have the concept of 'roundness' which we can think both without perceiving any round thing and in anticipation of those further round things which we might encounter. A concept gives order or direction to our thinking. Affect, by contrast, is the power to interrupt synthesis and order.) Just because our experience presents itself as a composite of sensible data and organising concepts does not mean that we cannot *think* the difference between the affective (the images that assault us) and the conceptual (the response and order we give to those images). For Deleuze, this means that we can take experience as it actually is (experience in its actual form) and differentiate it into its *virtual* components. Of course, we can never have a concept that does not occur through some sort of materiality or sensibility. We always have to have a word or sound from which we think the movement of concepts. Similarly, art does always have some sort of order, synthesis or meaning. (Deleuze was not arguing that art was just meaningless affect.) Indeed, art works by taking us back from composites of experience to the affects from which those synthesised wholes emerge. In cinema this is done in two ways, through the movement-image and the time-image.

Deleuze formed the concepts of the time-image and the movement-image in order to allow the event of cinema to transform all thinking. Recall that for Deleuze a concept is not a simple label but a creation that gives direction to thought. The concepts of the time-image and movement-image can now give us a clearer sense of this relation between concepts of philosophy and affects of art. Cinema's affects include those of the movement image, *so that movement itself is presented*. This is opposed to the interested and organised movement that is mapped by the eye as it finds its way home while driving or marks out those objects it will choose and grasp. The *concept* of this movement-image must therefore think what movement is in its radical and extreme forms, and not as it is mixed up with everyday life and concerns. For the most part, we experience images and movement from a point of view which includes meaning, purposes and our own concerns. Understanding movement itself means forming a concept of what movement is in its pure or virtual state: we should be able to think movement *as if* it were not the movement *of* some object *from* some fixed point. This is what a concept does: it does not label what is most common or frequent in day-to-day experience. It aims to think and imagine those extreme points where the singularities that make up experience are disclosed. We never *actually* see a world of pure movement; we always see movement in relation to fixed terms. But a concept takes us from the actual and everyday world to the virtual possibilities of that world; our world is made up of movement. The concept strives to think that movement from which we then organise a fixed and relatively mobile world. Understanding how Deleuze produces and uses these concepts helps to show the radical nature of his method. The whole task, as evidenced in his work on cinema, is that of discerning singularities: stepping back from our composed and ordered world and *thinking* the differences from which it is composed. Philosophy and art work in tandem here. Art presents singular affects and percepts, freed from organising and purposive viewpoints. Philosophy strives to think the possibility of these singularities: what *is* movement such that it produces all these differences? This means looking at exceptional rather than regular cases, so this is not a method that relies on common sense or looking at what is usual or typical. For the fact is, we rarely reach these moments of art where we are brought back from the order of common sense to the chaos of singularities. For Deleuze, though, the ethics of thinking in any form lies in how something works and what it can do, and not in any of its already given terms.

Thinking is not *generalising*. Instead of heaping up particulars and then coming up with some common feature, which would miss out all the differences (particular to general), Deleuze insists on the singular and Universal. The Universal captures the way each singular event becomes what it is, its specific power of being different. The Universal is not given, more or less, among all the examples; it is not a generalisation. A generalisation, for example, would take all the human beings we know and then list their common features as human: so if all the humans we knew happened to be over five feet tall we would have to say that humanity was defined in part by a certain height criterion. A Universal, on the other hand, does not just collate given qualities; it strives to discern what makes something specifically what it is. So, while all the humans we know may be five feet and over, we could still imagine someone as human who was four feet tall. But this would require that we think beyond what is given, and it would also require that we actively select what we take to be human: say, rationality or the capacity to think. The Universal is highly selective and virtual. In his work on cinema, therefore, Deleuze does not look at what cinema generally or typically is. He takes those forms of cinema that he sees as exceptional – such as the films of Orson Welles and Alain Resnais – and argues that they reveal what is cinematic about cinema. Not all human beings engage in radical thought, but thought is a uniquely human power. Not all films play with the very force of images, but the *power or potential* to free images from a fixed point of view is what makes cinema cinema. Cinema has its own way of creating differences. Just as human life can transform itself through thinking, so cinema transforms itself through the use of images. Seeing the Universal of the cinematic image would mean seeing how images can be different, irreducible to any common form. Creating concepts that allow us to think the Universal is, for Deleuze, crucial to the very ethics of life. If the Universal is what allows us to think the specific difference of any thing or mode of life, then the Universal is a way of freeing us from dogmas, preconceptions and prejudices. It leads us to think specific differences rather than generalities. The ethics of thinking lies in the opposite direction of reducing difference to common forms; we think when we differentiate. This is why, for Deleuze, we cannot base ethics on a common image of 'man' or 'human nature'. We cannot limit who or what we might become by any image of what we already are.

The advent of cinema might give us one form of *transversal* becoming: not a becoming that is grounded in a being and which simply unfolds itself through time, but a becoming that changes with each new encounter. Becoming is not just the unfolding of what something is. A thing (such as the human) can transform its whole way of becoming through an encounter with what it is not, in this case the camera. But this can only be so if we encounter the camera of cinema, not as something we already know, but as something that challenges us.

AFFECT AND DISORGANISED PERCEPTION

Crucially, Deleuze's books on cinema unfold his philosophy of time. This is more than just a 'philosophy'; for it is only if we rethink time, Deleuze argued, that we will be able to transform ourselves and our future. The capacity to rethink time, in different ways, is both the driving force of art and philosophy as well as being crucial to the becoming of life. Again, this is because the modes of thinking such as art, science and philosophy are not just idle cognitions or reflections;

they are the very medium through which we become. Second, cinema is not simply one mode through which we can confront time; cinema is not just another example or object for philosophy. How we do or think philosophy will be transformed by the advent of cinema. (And we might say the same for literature: Brett Easton Ellis's novel *Glamorama* (1999), for example, is written with the inclusion of multiple camera viewpoints.)

There is an important subsidiary point to be made here. If we accept that the invention and techniques of cinema allow us to think differently then we acknowledge that thought does not have its own inherent nature. Even machines, such as the technical possibilities of the camera, can transform thinking. Thinking, then, is not something that we can define once and for all; it is a power of becoming *and* its becoming can be transformed by what is not thinking's own – the outside or the unthought. Thinking is not something 'we' do; thinking happens to us, from without. There is a *necessity* to thinking, for the event of thought lies beyond the autonomy of choice. Thinking happens. At the same time, this necessity is also the affirmation of chance and freedom; we are not constrained by an order or pre-given end. True freedom lies in affirming the chance of events, not being deluded that we are 'masters' or that the world is nothing more than the limited perceptions we have of it. Freedom demands taking thinking, constantly, beyond itself.

Affect is crucial to this 'violence' of thinking (violence in the sense of something that happens to us beyond all morality). We can think of affect in terms of a form of pre-personal perception. I watch a scene in a film and my heart races, my eye flinches and I begin to perspire. Before I even think or conceptualise there is an element of response that is prior to any decision. Affect is *intensive* rather than *extensive*. Extension organises a world spatially, into distributed blocks. Ordered and synthesised perceptions give us an exterior world of varying extended objects, all mapped on to a common space, differing only in degree. Everyday vision takes this extensive form. I do not see a world of colours, tones and textures fluctuating from moment to moment. I see objects set apart from each other, stable through time and within a single and uniform extended space. Extension maps or synthesises the world in terms of presupposed purposes and intentions. (I go into my office and see the books that are there for me to read, the chair I will sit on, so on. I 'see' the world *as* a world of distinct functions,

affect is intensive

continuous through time.) <u>Affect is intensive because it happens to us, across us; it is not objectifiable and quantifiable as a thing that we then perceive or of which we are conscious</u>. Affect operates on us in divergent ways, differing in kind – the light that causes our eye to flinch, the sound that makes us start, the image of violence which raises our body temperature. Deleuze therefore refers to _intensities_.

If we see the world, usually, as a set of extended objects and as part of a uniform and measurable space, this is because we have synthesised intensities. <u>Intensities are not just qualities – such as redness – they are the becoming of qualities: say, the burning and wavering infrared light that we eventually see _as_ red</u>. For Deleuze, it is precisely because cinema composes images through time that it can present affects and intensities. It can disjoin the usual sequence of images – our usually ordered world with its expected flow of events – and allow us to perceive affects without their standard order and meaning. Perhaps the clearest cinematic use of divergent affects and intensities lies in the films of David Lynch, who combines desiring images of eroticism with sounds and acts of violence and decay. Images of visceral destruction that make the eye recoil are often combined with a soundtrack of lulling music. Unlike the perceived world of extended objects, which we order through a common space, intensities differ in kind. The proliferation of intensities in art destroys the image of a unified viewing subject who recognises a meaningful world that is there for us all. Intensities skew or scramble the faculties; the eye may desire while memory or judgement recoils in horror. Or, as in many of Lynch's images, the eye may be drawn and repelled concurrently.

In _Twin Peaks_ the corpse of Laura Palmer was at once an image of home-town American beauty, highly eroticised in its presentation. At the same time, the body was clearly a corpse with blue flesh and all the signs of death by drowning. It is in this and many other ways that cinema disengages images and affect from the unifying power of a single eye of judgement, producing affects that are at odds with the moral image of man. Now it may be the case that, in actual fact, we usually experience intensities from an organising point of view that imposes a common order. But the power of art to produce disruptive affect allows us to think intensities, to think the powers of becoming from which our ordered and composed world emerges. Cinema frees affect or the power of images from a world of coherent bodies differing only in degree, and opens up divergent lines of movement to differences in kind. Cinema short-circuits, if you like, the sensory-motor schema that governs our perception. For the most part, in everyday vision, we see and act, and we see in order to act. This is why we see a simplified world of extended objects, for we see what concerns us. In cinema the eye is disengaged from unified action, presented with images that prompt affective rather than cognitive responses.

For Deleuze this has political ramifications, for it helps to explain how we *as bodies* – respond and desire forms (such as Fascism) even when they would not be in our interest. We submit to repressive regimes, Deleuze argues, not because we are *mistaken* but because we desire certain affects. Think, for example, of the sensible intensities of political rallies: the anthems, the rhythm of speeches and marches, and the use of colour. These affective forces are not used to deceive us; here, we are not deluded by propaganda, but our bodies respond positively to these pre-personal 'investments'. Confronting the productive power of affect therefore allows us to confront what Deleuze refers to as the 'microperceptions' that make up who we are – not just the perceptions of the eye that sees and judges, but the disorganised perceptions of the life that pulses through our bodies.

MOVEMENT-IMAGE AND TIME

This returns us to the movement-image and its capacity to bring us to a rethinking of time. We have usually thought of time as the joining up of movement; time is what links, say, each step of my walk into a perceived line or unified action. But we can reverse this and say that time, far from being some sort of glue that holds distinct points of experience together, is an explosive force. Time is the power of life to move and become. Time produces movements, but the error has been to derive time from movements. Through affect art restores time's disruptive power. We no longer see life as some unified whole that goes through time; we see divergent becomings, movements or temporalities *from which* the whole would be derived. Instead of seeing each step of my walk as linked up through time, I could see a flowing movement – my continuous passage from one point to another – which I then cut up into distinct steps. I would see the walk not as a collection of steps, but as a process of change; for anyone who *has* tried to teach or learn walking by 'joining' one step to another would soon fall over!

Time is crucial to Deleuze's ethics of philosophy and the philosophical encounter with literature. And it is because cinema is that medium that enables us to rethink time that cinema is at the heart of our self-transformation. Our relation to time is ethical and political precisely because it is our way of living time (or our 'duration') which explains *the* problem of politics: how is it that our desire submits to its own repression? The very nature of time, for Deleuze, explains the way in which life can react against itself. Time creates certain 'internal illusions'. (We do not need to posit some deceiving enemy outside life – such as 'patriarchy', evil, or 'the capitalist' – to explain our repression.) From the complex flow of time we produce ordered wholes – such as the notion of the human self. We then imagine that this self *preceded or grounded the flow of time rather than being an effect of time*. The importance of overcoming this illusion cannot be overestimated. We tend to think of time as the connection of homogeneous or equivalent units within some already given whole; we think of a world in which there is time, or a world that then goes through time. We put being before becoming. We imagine time as a series of 'nows'. But time is not composed of 'nows' or units; we abstract the 'now' as some sort of being or thing from the becoming or flow of time. Time is not *extensive*; it is not the connection of distinct units. Time is *intensive*; always taking the form of different and divergent 'durations'. Imagine, for example, the difference between the duration of a plant, an animal and a human observer. The plant 'perceives' light, heat and water without any delay; it directly absorbs the light and so on. An animal introduces greater delay into perception; it can hesitate between which plant it might consume, or whether it will eat at all. So the speed or 'duration' of the animal gives it a certain degree of consciousness. Human beings, because of their power of thinking and memory, have a duration or speed which is not just more complex but extends to become a difference in kind. Concepts and affects can become disengaged from life and immediate action, producing a domain of thought that can bear a relation to time, that can think time.

Human duration is not just a mechanical or causal sequence of perceptions. Through memory, concepts, art and philosophy we can move backwards and forwards through the flow of time; we can think other durations, and we can disengage perception from the sensory-motor apparatus of prompted action. The animal feels hungry and eats, but a short-story writer can feel hunger and, rather than eat, present an image or fantasy of hunger. In 'The Hunger Artist' Franz Kafka (1961) explores a body that decides to delay the satisfaction of hunger; the artist *becomes* through the cultivation of hunger and starvation. It is by slowing down the response of the body that the 'artist' develops a sense and image of his body. Different beings – or what a thing is – are determined by different speeds. Humans can slow experience down in order to not act immediately, in order to select, decide and hesitate. The world of chosen actions is 'slower' than the immediate responses of micro-organisms. The world of philosophy might be described as one that moves at an imagined infinite speed: trying to encompass the whole of life at once. These different durations are only possible because time is *not* a sequence of one thing following another *within* some actual common ground. There is not a world that contains time; there is a flow of time, which produces 'worlds' or durations. Time is a virtual whole of divergent durations: different rhythms or pulsations of life which we can think or intuit. The everyday illusion is that life flows from one moment to the next and that we exist 'in' some general line of time. We can be freed from this illusion of a homogeneous, linear and undifferentiated time only by thinking of time as an intensive flow. This is where the power of cinema, among other things, opens life.

The movement-image gives us an indirect sense of this differing flow of time. First, we need to see the relation between time and movement in contrast with the day-to-day perception of recognition and common sense. We tend to spatialise time. We map or represent time by the movement of the sun across the sky, the hands moving around a clockface or some other moving body. In doing so we locate time *within* the world we perceive, within an actualised world of images. But how, we might ask, do we have this actual world? The world is not something within which time takes place; there are flows of time from which worlds are perceived. The durations of different becomings produce different worlds – including the inhuman worlds of plants and animals. We see a world of objects and tend to imagine time as the movement of an object from one point to another (such as the hands of a clock moving from one to twelve). But this world of moving *things* is only possible because we have reduced the complex flow of time, always differing from itself in different ways (such as the singular differences of light, sound, motion or texture) to a world of *beings*. Perception in its everyday form tends to fix itself as a point from which time and becoming are observed, so that there is one point from which time is relative.

We imagine each perception as a perception of an otherwise shared, stable and continuous world that is viewed *through time*. We forget that there is a temporal flow from which we have abstracted our point of perception. This is only possible if we have a single point of view – the point of view of judgement and action – and not a viewpoint that would include the movement or durations of the observed observers.

The movement-image of cinema takes us back from this homogeneous and ordered world of one single point of view to differing durations. Through the use of the camera we see time no longer as the line in which movement takes place but as a *divergent* pulsation or *difference* of incommensurable durations. One major technique for this is montage: the piecing together of different but conflicting sites of movement. In ordinary perception we homogenise time because we order the world from our own duration, imagining that there is one flow of time and that it is our own. Cinema, however, gives us a time which is 'impersonal, uniform, abstract, or imperceptible, which is "in" the apparatus' (Deleuze 1986: 1). The uniformity, here, refers to the fact that no point in time is privileged over any other; there is no observer who can govern and ground all others. But this uniformity and abstractness does not mean that time is undifferentiated; time is the very production of difference. By explicitly placing one point of view or flow of time alongside another cinematic montage shows us the divergence of time, or the different rhythms that make up the whole of time.

MOBILE SECTIONS

Cinema 'teaches us' that there are no moving bodies that take place in time. Rather, there are flows of time as movement and change from which we abstract distinct beings and bodies. The body is an effect or outcome of its movement and does not precede the flow of time through which it becomes. Time is always differing from itself. No two 'nows' are the same, and no two points of any movement or action are equivalent. Indeed, time is not a series of nows or points. In order to perceive time we spatialise it, cut it up into points or the various moments of a movement. But the true time of becoming is 'imperceptible'. When we perceive we reduce the complexity and difference of time – which is a virtual becoming that exceeds its perceived images – to an actual world of extended things. As we have seen, the art of cinema lies in freeing 'singular' images or becomings from a constituted whole, freeing perceptions from an ordering point of view. The movement-image presents 'mobile sections' – or movement in itself. Montage cuts and connects one flow of movement alongside another, but does not present these two movements from the single point of view of some ordering observer. We need to draw a distinction between Deleuze's claims for montage and the style of everyday narrative cinema. For the most part cinema in its popular form has a unified drama with central characters and a single plane of movement. The films that Deleuze refers to, such as the montage productions of Sergei Eisenstein (1898–1948), expand the visual scope beyond characters within a human drama. Such films produce movement-images that are not reducible to human actions or an intentional point of view. Montage collects points of movement as change or alteration: presenting a body that goes through decay, a body in growth, another body in transformation. There is no single line of time, nor movement within time. Time is imaged indirectly as the whole that produces all these different and incommensurable movements. Movement does not take place *within* time, because time is no longer some already given whole. Rather, time, as the force of movement, is always open and becoming in different ways. Movement does not just shift a body from one point to another (translation); in each block of movement bodies transform and become (variation). So each movement transforms the whole of time by producing new becomings:

> Movement always relates to a change, migration to a seasonal variation. And this is equally true of bodies: the fall of a body presupposes another one which attracts it, and expresses a change in the whole which governs them both. If we think of pure atoms, their movements which testify to a reciprocal action of all the parts of the substance, necessarily express modifications, disturbances, changes of energy in the whole ... beyond translation is vibration, radiation. Our error lies in believing that it is the any-element-whatevers, external to qualities which move. But the qualities themselves are pure vibrations which change at the same time as the alleged elements move.
>
> (Deleuze 1986: 8–9)

Cinema takes us away from the immobilised sections we impose on time to *mobile sections*. It presents the *moving* of movement, not a movement that is organised and fixed by some static point of view. Time is therefore presented indirectly. We sense time as that power of difference from which movement, as change rather than just shift in space, is propelled. We tend to impose relations on movements, seeing something as moving from one point to another, but before this relational and ordered whole there are *singular* movements or variations. A leaf falls and dies, withering and losing colour; this is part of the life and duration of the plant, its own specific rhythm. Elsewhere a bird crosses the sky, migrating in order to breed, and the movement of the bird crosses the movement of the clouds that are about to condense to produce rain. Each movement is not just a change of place within a whole but a becoming in which the movement is a transformation of the body which moves, a body being nothing other than its movements. The human observer can only perceive these three becomings from her own duration, but a camera could present movement across movement, could juxtapose movements: mobile sections. We would then get a sense of time as a whole of differing series of becomings beyond our organising point of view. The art of montage presents these mobile sections. Each movement bears its own rhythm and pulsation. Any system that relates all these differing durations into one single or privileged whole would be externally imposed, for the true whole of time is not an already given plane within which movements take place. It is rather an 'Open whole', transformed with each singular movement: 'if the whole is not givable it is because it is the Open, and because its nature is to change constantly, or to give rise to something new, in short, to endure' (Deleuze 1986: 9). Enduring or duration is not the connection of a series of points that are all pretty much the same; it is a flow of differing difference. With each movement what a thing *is* changes, thus producing new possibilities for movement and becoming. In the cinema of the movement-image we have frames which organise sets of images. In addition to this collection of frames, there is also the out-of-field. On the one hand this whole which we do not see is just the actual collection of sets of frames. On the other hand, what we do not see, or what is not given in montage, is the *virtual* whole: all the tendencies of movement or becoming from which cinema has 'cut' various sets of movement:

> there is always out-of-field, even in the most closed image. And there are always simultaneously the two aspects of the out-of-field, the actualisable relation with other sets, and the virtual relation with the whole.

> (Deleuze 1986: 18)

It is the movement itself which is decomposed and recomposed. It is decomposed according to the elements between which it plays in a set: those which remain fixed, those to which movement is attributed, those which produce or undergo such simple or divisible movement according to the whole whose change it expresses.

(Deleuze 1986: 20–1)

A camera moves in one direction across one moving body, from left to right. It then stops and moves down across another body, from height to depth. Time is no longer perceived from a static point of view watching events go by. The cuts of cinema, playing mobile sections alongside each other, give as an indirect image of time as a constantly differing whole, open to variation and multiple durations.

CINEMA, POSSIBILITIES AND POLITICS

It is in modern or post-war film that Deleuze argues for the true realisation of cinema in the time-image. Before looking at this in detail we should perhaps see just what Deleuze is *doing* with cinema and how his approach to cinema discloses something about his method in general. There is a problem with talking about 'method' in Deleuze, simply because his whole approach to life and thinking set itself against any idea that we should approach problems with ready-made schemas, questions or systems. We need to allow thought to open itself up to possibilities that lie outside thinking. Philosophy, especially, ought to be creative and responsive, forming its questions through what it encounters. And art is the very opposite of method; art is not a form we impose on experience. Art is allowing the anarchy of experience to free itself from forms and methods. If Deleuze has a method it is that we should never have *a* method, but should allow ourselves to *become* in relation to what we are seeking to understand. On the odd occasion when Deleuze did refer to method he used the word 'intuition'. This means going beyond the perception of something in its actual form to the virtual components that make it up. Through intuition we see the flow of time beyond spatialised images, or we see the movements of thinking beyond fixed meanings. We see the *genetic element* in all life – the process of difference from which different beings are actualised. (So, 'genetics' in its narrow sense – the understanding of the potential events which are actualised in each of our bodies – is part of a much broader *genesis* of time. After all, we would not have genetic differentiation if there were not the flow of time, which produces all manner of difference.) Deleuze's method, therefore, looks for what he refers to as the 'ideal genetic element', not some actually given thing but the process or power of difference that produces differentiated terms.

When Deleuze looks at cinema his approach is diametrically opposed to the usual methods of cultural studies or literary theory. To begin with, his method is not interpretive. We should not, he argued, look for the meaning or message conveyed by cinematic images. Second, we should not look at cinematic images as representations. It is common to complain that cinema offers 'unrepresentative' images of women, for example, and so the remedy for cinema would be to be more realistic. But cinema, for Deleuze, is not about representing a world we already have; it creates new worlds. We should not criticise the way cinema constructs 'stereotypes', reinforces everyday opinions or lulls us into a false sense of reality. Cinema may well do these things. But for Deleuze philosophy as intuition is not about seeing the limited forms of life; it is about recognising the potential for transformation and becoming in all life. So we should see cinema for what it can or might do, and not for what it is. For this reason there is a 'high-culture' emphasis in all Deleuze's work. What philosophy or art *is* is what it can *do*, even if most of what passes for 'culture' or art never realises its potential and is hardly worthy of the name. The time-image, which expresses the force of cinema's potential, may be so rare as to be only thinkable in its pure form, never fully actualisable. The time-image gives us time itself, no longer spatialised or derived from movement.

If we think of the very possibility of genesis of cinema, or how cinema becomes, then we can think of 'durations' beyond our own. For Deleuze, this is the power or Idea of the time-image. Because we perceive the world from our own interested viewpoint we usually locate all other durations within our own. We experience time as a single progressing line composed of equivalent moments. And we perceive other beings as within this general time. We perceive the plant as an extended object, not as a process that 'perceives' other pulsations of heat, light and moisture. We perceive other persons as bodies, like ours, and within our world; we don't perceive the different 'world' of the other, their own duration. There is, Deleuze insists, a multiplicity of human durations and inhuman durations. Only if we think beyond our spatialising and ordering viewpoint can we think these other durations. The early cinema of the movement-image does not present duration *itself*. However, by destroying the position of a fixed observer who synthesises time into a static whole, we get an indirect sense of a whole composed of different durations. Instead of there being things in space which then move, with time being the totality within which movement takes place, there are multiple movements. It is from these mobile sections that perception then fixes or abstracts actual objects. Cinema shares with painting, and the method of intuition, the capacity to perceive movement from the point of view of the moving thing itself (Deleuze 1986: 23), rather than a detached external observer. By presenting divergent movements time is articulated, or seen as differing. This time is an *effective* time – a time that produces difference. This is how Deleuze explains montage:

> What amounts to montage, in itself or in something else, is the indirect image of time, of duration. Not a homogeneous time or a spatialised duration . . . , but an effective duration and time which flow from the articulation of the movement-image.
>
> (Deleuze 1986: 29)

For Deleuze this use of montage had a political function that had nothing to do with political 'messages' or meanings. And this is crucial for Deleuze's entire emphasis on politics as 'pre-personal'. Before there are persons who debates issues and *interests*, time has to be composed into distinct beings or identities. Both philosophy and art decompose or intuit these micro-perceptions, showing how 'our' world is synthesised from flows of images. Politics emerges from the very form or synthesis of experience. We can only radicalise politics by de-forming experience away from 'meanings' (or ordered wholes) to its effective components (those singularities which produce meaning). Montage, for example, allows the inhuman durations of matter to be perceived. This gives us history – not a history as human drama, but histories of the processes of matter outside thinking and ordinary perception. If we no longer see the human point of view as single and all-determining then we can get an indirect sense of time, or history, as a shaping force. We can be brought up against our material and historical formation. It is the *inhuman* eye of the camera that liberates us from a fixed and moral notion of man, allowing us to assess the larger material forces that have constituted us:

> The eye is not the too-immobile human eye; it is the eye of the camera, that is an eye in matter, a perception such as it is in matter, ... The correlation between a non-human matter and a super-human eye is the dialectic itself, because it is also the identity of a community of matter and a communism of man. And montage itself constantly adapts the transformations of movements in the material universe to the interval of movement in the eye of the camera, rhythm.

(Deleuze 1986: 40)

In *Cinema 1* Deleuze describes a mode of dialectical cinema that is achieved through montage: the connection of different and divergent historical movement such that there is not a uniform flow of time so much as different durations, each with their own power. 'Time' is

DIALECTICS

Dialectics has a long philosophical history going back to the Ancient Greeks who allowed different opinions to encounter each other in order for the truth to emerge through a dialectic or confrontation. Dialectic worked through negation: by assessing various views that were deemed to be inadequate the argument would arrive at the truth. In modern philosophy the dialectic is associated with Hegel, who argued that the contradictions of life needed to be confronted through a dialectical method that would perceive their underlying identity. It is when our concepts seem inadequate or contradictory that we are compelled to reassess our relation to the real world. What appears as contradictory or as other than thought needs to be rendered rational and comprehended within thought. The argument for *historical* dialectic that followed Hegel tried to show that social conflicts and human suffering can only be understood by an awareness of those forces (such as history) which appear to be incomprehensible or negative. Deleuze argues against a dialectic that would place contradictions together in order to reveal some final truth, but he insisted on a 'superior dialectic' that would allow differences and contradictions to remain in tension: this would not reveal an underlying truth or identity. It would disclose difference and becoming.

presented as the limit of all these different durations; we get particular moments of history and conclude that history is just the unity of
all these conflicts.

Deleuze's 'dialectical' politics is one in which the camera gives us
an indirect sense of history, history not as the inevitable unfolding of
some unchanging human essence, but history as materialist, the very
motion of matter. (Deleuze will, however, insist in going beyond
dialectic or beyond the relation *between* man and matter. This will be
achieved in the time-image, where the distinction between human and
inhuman flows from a more open whole of duration.) In this dialectical use of cinema, it is in our engagement, reaction and interaction
with the rhythms of nature that we become who we are. This dialectical politics goes some way, for Deleuze, in freeing human life from
fixed or 'moral' images of what humanity is, and opens thought up
for a future. Deleuze was also critical of the dialectic, whereby something (such as human life) becomes in relation to what it is *not*. The
problem is that this dialectical difference begins from an opposition
between human life and the material forces that shape it. We see time
in its effects, after the event, from the human point of view in relation
to 'other' durations.

THE DIRECT IMAGE OF TIME

If we *really* confront time or duration, however, we see a single flow
of difference or becoming: not the becoming *of* moving things, nor
the becoming of human life in relation to other movements. Time is
a becoming without ground, without foundation. The time-image takes
us away from the *negativity* of the dialectic. The dialectic is negative
because it can only view difference or becoming as *other than* (or as
what transforms) fixed being. In the cinema of the movement-image
the flow of time is sensed as that which lies above and beyond any
of the divergent movements. In the time-image we sense duration
directly, not derived from movement. Unlike the dialectic, its becoming is positive: for we confront becoming itself, not as an indirect
whole of all the composed mobile sections. And this non-dialectical or
positive becoming also has a different political orientation. It does not
just free us from fixed images by indicating the flow of history from
which we have emerged; it presents the creative flow of time as
becoming or the opening to the future.

Just *how* the time-image could do this takes us back to the heart of Deleuze's project. It is not that there are things or beings which then move or become. Life is movement and becoming from which distinct things are actualised. The world is a flow of images or perceptions; these are not yet images *of* some underlying being. Only distinct perceptions fix this flux of images into a world of 'things':

> Let us call the set of what appears 'Image'. We cannot ever say that one image acts on another or reacts to another. There is no moving body [*mobile*] which is distinct from executed movement. There is nothing moved which is distinct from the received movement. Every thing, that is to say every image, is indistinguishable from its actions and reactions; this is universal variation.
>
> (Deleuze 1986: 58)

My perception of this thing as red, for example, relies on me reducing the complex and differing waves of light into a homogeneous perceived colour and an extended object. A different eye would perceive more complex differences, or less difference. Each point of perception is also, in itself, a becoming. Any eye that sees is already a flow of life, anticipating a future and propelled from a past. We see a world of moving things, but this is only possible because we have abstracted from a whole of movement; we neglect the movements in our own becoming and we neglect the differences that do not concern us. Above and beyond any perceiver-perceived *relation* there is a general, impersonal and anonymous plane of becoming. There can only be a relation – one point of response to another – because of an effective time which produces the very power of becoming. In contrast to the dialectical approach, where we see the limits of each thing's duration *in relation* to other durations, Deleuze demands that we think duration, difference or becoming *itself*, independent of its actualised forms of external relations. Dialectic, for example, can gesture to a time which lies outside human order by, say, presenting grander images of decay and growth that go beyond human purpose: in so doing it allows us to think of a time beyond our own. But cinema can do more than just show us the limits of our own historical time; it can present inhuman durations. The human eye cannot actually perceive the growth and becoming of a plant, but we are probably all familiar with a documentary technique that fixes on a plant or insect over a period of days and then speeds this up so that we are actually brought to what is usually imperceptible. Now, imagine this more radically, with a camera that can use different speeds and sequences that grasp the imperceptible but without speeding them up to restore us to narrative order. Our ordered flow of images in time would become a flow of time itself, for there would be processes of perception that were not recognised as processes *of* some object within our world.

Some people might object that this is simply not possible. How could we think pure becoming that is not the becoming *of* some thing? Deleuze's philosophy or method lies in this problem (and a problem is only productive if it *does not* have an evident answer, or if it has an element of impossibility). Deleuze offers several responses to this problem of a pure becoming. The first is in relation to cinema and the time-image. The time-image, the direct presentation of becoming itself, can be what cinema works towards, its *Idea*. Deleuze takes this notion of the Idea from the eighteenth-century philosopher Immanuel Kant (1724–1804) on whom Deleuze wrote an extended study which was published in French in 1963 (Deleuze 1984). An Idea is a concept pushed beyond any possible experience. Let us say that we have the concept of cause, such that we experience our world in terms of causes and effects. If we extend this concept beyond experience we can think of some ultimate or first cause, a cause that is not the effect of some prior cause. This might give us the Idea of God. But this can only be an Idea, for to experience something it has to be placed within the order of time; we cannot *experience* the beginning of time but we can *think* it. We cannot experience a first cause because to experience something is to give it a place within a causal sequence. But while we cannot know or experience a first cause *actually*, we can think it. An Idea extends the concepts through which we think the world to a virtual point beyond the world. Deleuze uses this notion of the Idea throughout his work. The Idea is the extension to the nth or infinite power of an actual possibility. We see this or that actually differing thing, but we can think difference as such, as the very becoming of life. For Deleuze this Idea of difference is not just something *we* can think; it is life itself. For the key point of the Idea is that it is not given, fully presented or givable; it is the power for any series to extend itself beyond the actual.

Cinema has the time-image as its Idea. At its most powerful cinema presents not this or that movement but the power of difference from which we discern movement. Cinema is not representation; it is an event of intuition which goes beyond the actually given to the Idea of the image. Cinema sees, not a world of things, not even a distinct world, but the movement of imaging from which any perceived world is possible. But it only achieves this in the time-image.

The time-image is operated by 'irrational cuts'. Everyday experience synthesises or connects images into ordered wholes. Cinema works in the opposite direction, breaking experience down into the irrational (or not yet unified or conceptualised) singularities. We are not just, as in the movement-image, given competing points of view of differing mobile sections, we are freed from viewpoint. This can be achieved, for example, by incongruent voices played over disconnected visual images, removing a sense of reference. In the time-image the image is no longer perceived as an image *of* this or that. It is the image in its singularity, so we see imaging as such, not yet incorporated into a viewpoint, not yet ordered into a line of time. The irrational cuts do not allow images to link together to form moving things, and in so doing we are presented with imaging itself, both in its production of movement and its production of connection:

> It took the modern cinema to re-read the whole of cinema as already made up of aberrant movements and false continuity shots. The direct time-image is the phantom which has always haunted the cinema, but it took modern cinema to give a body to this phantom. This image is virtual, in opposition to the actuality of the movement-image.
>
> (Deleuze 1989: 41)

This is not a cinema of the actual – the world as it is – but of the virtual; it presents the imaging and connection processes from which any world could be perceived: 'With the cinema, it is the world which becomes its own image, and not an image which becomes world' (Deleuze 1986: 57).

CINEMATIC PHILOSOPHY

For Deleuze this becoming-image is what makes cinema philosophical and philosophy cinematic. Cinema, like art or literature, is philosophical not because it conveys ideas or messages or offers us some theory of the world. Cinema produces new possibilities for the human eye and perception; it creates new affects. We can experience flows and connections of images through time that are not perceived from a fixed point and that are not synthesised to form wholes. Cinema itself is not conceptual, but it presents a challenge to our concepts: Deleuze forms the philosophical concepts of the time-image in response to cinema. In this way, cinema has allowed philosophy, and thinking, to become. We could say, then, that philosophy's relation to *any* art is not that of offering a theory of art or aesthetics, but rather that philosophy responds to the new perceptive forces or affects which art allows. What philosophy does in this response, with its creation of new concepts, is to open up a future for thinking. In Deleuze's case it is perhaps cinema that prompts the problem of difference in itself, the problem of the virtual power of difference beyond any of its actual images:

> if the cinema goes beyond perception, it is in the sense that it reaches to the *genetic element* of all possible perception, that is, the point which changes, and which makes perception change, the differential of perception itself.
>
> (Deleuze 1989: 83)

> Camera-consciousness raises itself to a determination which is no longer formal or material, but genetic and differential.
>
> (Deleuze 1989: 85)

SUMMARY

Life is a flow of time or becoming, a whole of interactions or 'perceptions'. Each event of perception opens up to its own world. Above and beyond all these actualised worlds there is a virtual whole composed of a multiplicity of durations. In cinema we free the perception of the world from its fixed and ordering viewpoint. This is done in two waves. Early cinema reaches the movement-image. Instead of bodies that move from one point to another, we see movement itself or mobile sections. Modern cinema goes further with the time-image. Images are no longer connected to form logical sequences; by the use of irrational cuts we are given an image of time itself. This time is not a simple linear progression from one point to another, but a divergent and differentiating becoming. Cinema, therefore, has the power of taking thought beyond its own fixed images of itself and the world; we can think of images that are no longer images *of* some being.

3

MACHINES, THE UNTIMELY AND DETERRITORIALISATION

One of the key ideas that runs throughout Deleuze's work and which links his philosophy of time to an ethics is the concept of the machine. In this chapter we will look at how Deleuze moves away from humanist and organicist models in order to think a becoming and time that has no ground or foundation. This ties in with his insights on cinema, for cinema was already a 'machinic' becoming – a series of images freed from the human eye and located observer. Deleuze uses this concept of the machine to rethink ethics. We tend to begin our thinking from some presupposed whole: such as man, nature or an image of the universe as an interacting organism with a specific end. This allows our ethics to be *reactive*: we form our ethics on the basis of some pre-given unity. The machine by contrast allows for an *active* ethics, for we do not presuppose an intent, identity or end. Deleuze uses the machine to describe a production that is immanent: not the produc-tion *of* something *by* someone – but production for the sake of production itself, an ungrounded time and becoming. In this chapter we will look at how the radical and open nature of time can be thought of 'machinically' and how this allows Deleuze to form a new mode of ethics and reading. The idea of deterritorialisation, which runs through Deleuze and Guattari's work, is directly related to the thought of the machine. Because a machine has no subjectivity or organising centre it *is* nothing more than the connections and productions it makes; it is what it does. It therefore has no home or ground; it is a constant process of deterritorialisation, or becoming other than itself.

In *Anti-Oedipus* and *A Thousand Plateaus* Deleuze and Guattari use a terminology of machines, assemblages, connections and productions. In *Anti-Oedipus* they insist that the machine is not a metaphor and that life is *literally* a machine. This is crucial to Deleuze's ethics. An *organism* is a bounded whole with an identity and end. A _mechanism_ is a closed machine with a specific function. A _machine,_ however, is nothing more than its connections; it is not made by anything, is not for anything and has no closed identity. So they are using 'machine' here in a specific and unconventional sense. Think of a bicycle, which obviously has no 'end' or intention. It only works when it is connected with another 'machine' such as the human body; and the production of these two machines can only be achieved through connection. The human body becomes a cyclist in connecting with the machine; the cycle becomes a vehicle. But we could imagine different connections producing different machines. The cycle becomes an art object when placed in a gallery; the human body becomes an 'artist' when connected with a paintbrush. The images we have of closed machines, such as the self-contained organism of the human body, or the efficiently autonomous functioning of the clock mechanism, are effects and illusions of the machine. There is no aspect of life that is not machinic; all life only works and *is* insofar as it connects with some other machine.

We have already seen the importance Deleuze gives to the camera; it is important as a machine because it shows how human thought and life can become and transform through what is inhuman. By insisting that the machine is not a metaphor Deleuze and Guattari move away from a representational model of language. If the concept of machine were a metaphor, then we could say that we have life as it is, and then the figure of machine to imagine, represent or picture life. But for Deleuze and Guattari there is no present life outside of its connections. We only have representations, images or thoughts *because* there have been 'machinic' connections: the eye connects with light, the brain connects with a concept, the mouth connects with a language. Life is not about one privileged point – the self-contained mind of 'man'-representing some inert outside world. Life is a proliferation of machinic connections, with the mind or brain being one (sophisticated) machine among others.

Neither philosophy, nor art, nor cinema represent the world; they are events through which the movement of life becomes. What makes

machinic becoming

philosophy and art *active* is their capacity to become not just *mechanistically*, being caused by outside events, but *machinically*. A mechanism is a self-enclosed movement that merely ticks over, never transforming or producing itself. A machinic becoming makes a connection with what is not itself in order to transform and maximise itself. In the case of cinema and the time-image, as we saw in the last chapter, the human eye connects with the eye of the camera; this then creates perceptions or images *beyond the human*. In the time-image we are confronted with becoming itself and this presents us with a challenge – the same challenge that runs through art and philosophy but in different ways – to become worthy of becoming, worthy of the powers of difference that flow through us and beyond us (Deleuze 1990: 149–50). Philosophy and art provide the power of the *untimely*. Life is not just the progression of ordered sequences from some already given set of possibilities. Each branching out of difference creates the expansion of possibility, so the 'end' of life is not given, there is no goal towards which life is striving. But there is an 'internal' or effective striving in life: to enhance its power, to maximise what it can do. This is achieved not by all events leading up to an end, but by the creation of ever divergent ends, creating more and more series or 'lines' of becoming. In *A Thousand Plateaus* Deleuze and Guattari refer to life's production of 'lines of flight', where mutations and differences produce not just the progression of history but disruptions, breaks, new beginnings and 'monstrous' births. This is also the *event:* not another moment within time, but something that allows time to take off on a new path. Cinema is an event for it allows an image of time, not just as a series of moving images, but time as the power to produce the very becoming of images.

It is this thought of the machine that also allows for an emphasis on the virtual dimension of time. In his cinema books Deleuze had shown that the disruption of images and sequences can present a time that is *not our own*. Instead of seeing time as the coherent series of images from my own viewpoint, I am presented with other sequences, other times, other lines of becoming. This opens up to a sense of time beyond my perception, while the camera allows us to think an inhuman perception; this gives us an image of time beyond what we *actually* perceive and live. Time is a virtual whole; it is never given or perceived (actualised) by any single observer or collection of observers. We need to think time machinically: not as the eternal whole of an already given universe that is one present organism, but as an *open* whole of what may happen through unthought-out and unintended connections and proliferations.

On the one hand, Deleuze's insistence on the virtual power of time seems to be an ahistorical or anti-historical philosophy. It is certainly the case that even when Deleuze wrote histories of philosophy or the history of capitalism (in *Anti-Oedipus* and *A Thousand Plateaus*) he does not see history as a meaningful sequence. Nor can history explain the emergence or event of art and philosophy. But Deleuze wrote a history that was 'geological' as well as 'genealogical'. In genealogy he traced the improbable birth of events; the political idea of 'man', for example, is the result of reducing tyrannical images of the despot or ruler to the bourgeois image of the universal citizen. In geology he shows how life and time become in a multiplicity of layers: genetic, chemical, geological and cultural events all produce different strata or 'plateaus' of life. There is no single history within which all life might be ordered. The idea of a geology suggests that there is a distribution, a drawing of lines, a plane of differences, a number of planes or plateaus which constitute *life*, and that this number of plateaus cannot be located *within* the unity of a subject.

As we have seen with the time-image, cinema is at its most cinematic not when it is presenting ordered temporal narratives, such as historical epics or dramas with historical 'contexts'. Instead, cinema becomes affirmative when it frees us from the idea of time as a connected order or sequence. In the time-image we do not see time as a logical connection or progression but as interval, disruption or difference; cinema presents the way things do *not* hang together through images in states of variation without organising observers or subjects. Deleuze refers to this as a 'deterritorialisation' of the image. Deterritorialisation frees a possibility or event from its actual origins (Deleuze 1986: 96). Deterritorialisation produces an image of 'pure affect' (96); there is a sensation that is not referred to any specific body or place. Beyond cinema, both deterritorialisation and affect are crucial concepts for Deleuze and they carry us to the heart of what he refers to as the untimely. Life, for Deleuze, is not some general homogeneous matter, that is then differentiated or goes through time, but a whole of singularities. Each point in life becomes in its own way with its own rhythm, producing its own 'refrain'. (More accurately, we would not speak of located 'points' of life, because there are no fixed points or territories. We might rather, as Deleuze and Guattari do, refer to 'blocks of becoming' or tendencies to become in specific ways.) Plants, animals, humans and atoms all possess different powers of becoming. Deterritorialisation occurs when an event of becoming escapes or detaches from its original territory. Think of the way humans organise or *territorialise* themselves through language. Language can then become inhuman or *deterritorialised* in art: no longer meaningful, controllable or recognisable. Or, think of the time-image. It is the human production of the sequence of cinematic movements that gives us a linear time; but the image can become deterritorialised by producing illogical sequences taking us beyond human temporality.

'Pure affect' is also a deterritorialisation. If I perceive red I usually do so by referring it to the redness *of* some thing, and from some interested and organising point of view. Imagine a cinema that presented colours in such a disorganised and disconnected way that colour could no longer be attributed to a specific thing or object in space, and where we would get a sense of colour itself, not *as perceived* (actually) but as what is produced or given from a virtual flow of light. This would be the becoming, pure affect or deterritorialisation of colour, the becoming-colour of colour. I see the singularity of red, red as it would be, not here and now, but in any object whatever:

> In opposition to a simply coloured image, the colour-image does not refer to a particular object, but absorbs all that it can: it is the power which seizes all that happens within its range, or the quality common to completely different objects. There *is* a symbolism of colours, but it does not consist in a correspondence between a colour and an affect (green of hope . . .). Colour is on the contrary the affect itself, the virtual conjunction of all the objects which it picks up.
>
> (Deleuze 1986: 118)

There can also be non-sensible affects: the camera focuses on a knife and we 'see' its power to cut – not from the point of view of a threatened observer (so, not as in a suspense thriller such as Hitchcock's *Psycho*). The non-sensible affect is a power of expression; we see not what *is* but what might become, the possible 'cutting' of the knife. And such a becoming would be an *event*: two bodies would meet in time, such as the knife and flesh, and produce an event above those bodies: the wound or the injury. The world of these powers of expression or powers of becoming is, for Deleuze, the incorporeal world of _sense_. Sense expresses not what something actually is but its power to become. This is why language is one way in which life produces sense, for words allow us to take a thing and place it in virtual connections with other things. Sense is a power of _incorporeal transformation_; whether I refer to the cut (actual) body as 'injured', 'scarred' or 'punished' will alter what it is in its incorporeal or virtual being. Sense is an event, producing new lines of becoming. And sense is also the power of the untimely. Bodies do not just join together in causal sequences that can be mapped out in advance, for the becoming of sense produces whole new lines of becoming. When a court refers to a body as a 'criminal' or when a social scientist 'discovers' a new class or personality 'syndrome', then new histories become possible. Sense allows certain powers of becoming to be given _being_; it is sense that produces national, racial and sexual identities.

An _active_ philosophy affirms this production of sense as a _deterritorialisation_, as the way in which bodies transform and become. A _reactive_ philosophy, by contrast, refers sense, affect and becoming back to some original being. We imagine, for example, that there _is_ something like the 'criminal mind' or 'femininity' that only needs time in order to become; we see history as the simple unfolding or _becoming of_ some prior being. But if, following Deleuze, we acknowledge that life is the dynamic interaction of affects and a constant becoming-other, then it would be naïve to see history as a logical flow or meaningful sequence, for the future is not given in the present. New powers of becoming are always being produced. Indeed, the _only_ thing that returns or is repeated is the power of difference. This is how Deleuze refers to the idea of 'eternal return', an idea which he gathers from Nietzsche. Time is eternal only in its power to always produce the new, over and over again – with no origin and no end. The only constant in time, the only 'Same', is the power of not remaining the same. Affect is the expression of this impersonal becoming, precisely because affect is an event that is not grounded in any agent or subject. It is not the becoming _of_ some being but a becoming that is nothing more than its own distinct difference and flow. This model of difference, this attempt to think difference and becoming, before being and identity relies on a new relation between quality and quantity. For Deleuze, difference in quantity is not the simple increment of identical units. A true increase in quantity changes what something is, so we need to see quantity temporally, as a becoming more or less that is truly an event of change. Unlike a spatial object where more or less still leaves the thing as the same – a bigger or smaller red object is still a red object – a change in quantity of affect changes the quality. More or less light changes the redness of a colour; more or less sensation determines whether there is pleasure or pain. Deleuze therefore refers to affect as 'dividual', such that it has no identity or individuality independent of its specific quantity or division:

> The affect is impersonal and is distinct from every individual State of things: it is none the less *singular*, and can enter into singular combinations and conjunctions with other affects. The affect is indivisible and without parts; but the singular combinations that it forms with other affects form in turn an indivisible quality, which will only be divided by changing the quality quantitatively (the 'dividual'). The affect is independent of all determinate space-time; but it is none the less created in a history which produces it as the expressed and the expression of a space or a time, of an epoch or a milieu (this is why the affect is the 'new' and new affects are ceaselessly created, notably by the work of art).
>
> (Deleuze 1986: 98–9)

If affect is not the perception *of* something by an organising observer, but the presentation of a force of something to-be-perceived from points beyond our own, then affect opens the *line* of time to disruption, giving an 'untimely' time or a time 'out of joint'.

THE UNTIMELY

Once we free life from its organicist or foundational models, where every becoming is grounded on an origin, end or order, we are open to rethinking time. Affect is crucial, here, precisely because Deleuze frees affect from being. It is not that there are persons who *then* feel and perceive, or a life that then has qualities. Life is a dynamic swarm of affects, of interactions, encounters or purely machinic connections and productions. It is from affects that distinct beings are formed. A body makes certain affective connections, its mouth is drawn to a breast, its eye directed to a face, its hands attracted to tools. These *investments* or connections create what it is to be human. The body is produced through time, through becoming. There is, then, a history and politics of affect. It is a history that attends to *disruptions*. It is also what Deleuze refers to as the untimely, monstrous or violent power of art and philosophy. Neither art nor philosophy are about representing a world that is already there, they are about making connections or becoming 'desiring machines'.

For Deleuze, the history of philosophy or literature is *not* about placing texts in their 'contexts'. It is not, for example, about looking at how Shakespeare reflected or even contested the Elizabethan worldview. Art and philosophy are untimely because they have the power to create whole new lines of time or 'lines of flight'. The *art* of Shakespeare does not lie in his representative response to his own time but in his capacity to conceive time differently. Consider the way his history plays take the notion of history as a natural and divine progression (the ordained sequence of true and destined kings) and introduce another notion of history whereby characters decide to act *as if* they were divine. Kings and rulers who express destiny, fate and the timelessness of time (Macbeth, Richard II, Caesar) are displaced by those who see time as performance and production. History becomes an act, a production or a creation, and power is won by those, such as Henry IV, who can produce and create themselves as historical figures. Shakespeare's history plays and tragedies do not just chart, represent or contest events within history; they open a new experience of history. What they express are not occurrences within time, but time as performance, time as open to the future: time as drama, not as destiny.

Today, if we were to repeat or film Shakespeare the art would lie not just in re-narrating the characters or events but in grasping anew this affect or expression of time. We might, for example, film *Richard II* in an apocalyptic or post-nuclear landscape, playing off the sense of history as human performance with the possible end to all human time. Repeating Shakespeare would demand repeating all the infidelity to context that opened Shakespeare's own time. We would not be repeating the *meaning* of Shakespeare's work but its untimely power: its power to disrupt our present and the sense of time as continuity, in the 'same' way that it once disrupted the sense of time as divine order:

> To reach a repetition which saves, or which changes life, beyond good and evil, would it not be necessary to break with the order of impulses, to undo the cycles of time, reach an element which would be like a true 'desire', or like a choice constantly beginning again.
>
> (Deleuze 1986: 133)

Reading a work, for Deleuze, is affirming its untimely affects, not just the way it responded to a context, but its capacity to take us beyond all context. If a work disrupts 'our' notion of time and history then it is at once located within an epoch and at the same time expresses a new time and new epoch. The time-image of the cinema, for example, is one of Deleuze's untimely concepts. Cinema is at once the most popular and widespread medium of images at the same time as it is capable of transforming the whole notion of the image. It is through cinema that we often get the idea that the world is simply present, ready to be re-presented in a realist cinema where we can recognise ourselves and our world, but it is also in the cinema that we have a disruption of this sense of the shared present. It is in the time-image that we are taken from the relative flow of time which is the same from one observer to another, to the *different* durations depending on the different speeds or rhythms of perception. Time opens out on to the eternal: on to the flux of images and affects from which we become.

THE NEW AND REPETITION

The time-image is therefore new for our time. It disturbs our unified, linear or spatialised sense of time. But newness, for Deleuze, is not just the shock of the new that has its contextual effect and then passes away; the new is eternally new. The newness of art does not lie in its shock-effect, such that once we get used to modern cinema or modernism there would no longer be any value. To think of the new as a 'blip' within time is to think of time as a sequence that has its disruptions but then flows on. The new does not occur within time; true time is newness itself, the eternal production of transformation. For this reason it is always possible to read the production of the new in any moment of time, and Deleuze's works on philosophers did just that. What made David Hume a new thinker? What is it to *create* philosophy? These were questions that Deleuze used to approach Hume, one of the seemingly most conservative philosophers of conventional history (Deleuze 1991). Similarly, reading a literary text is not about placing it within its context, nor about seeing how it was once new. Why would we still read Shakespeare if he were only imaginative or affective for Renaissance England? Reading Shakespeare ought not to be a study in the history of ideas; it should allow us to re-confront the formation, genesis or creation of ideas. Philosophy produces concepts that allow us to think of the very genesis of concepts; and art produces affects that help us to think of the very newness of affect. If we were to *repeat* Shakespeare today then we would not don Elizabethan costumes, rebuild the Globe and take ourselves back in time – whatever that means – to a past that remains unchanged. Repeating the past always transforms the past, for the past is as much in production as the present. Each performance or memory of the past opens the past anew. Repeating Shakespeare's *Richard II* would mean producing the play today with all the power and newness that it had for its time. Looking at history, then, is not looking at a series of ideas that follow each other in time; it is looking at the different ways in which time takes eventful turns. We might produce *Richard II*, at the extreme, not as a history play but as a cyber-play, as a production of images of time and history: a *Richard II* using techniques from video-games, MTV or web-sites? To do so would be to use the past to challenge the future; later productions would also rethink time and history, using each event of the new to rethink what it is to be new.

When Deleuze describes his own philosophy as untimely he suggests that we should look to the past, not to find out what it was, but to allow the force of past problems, questions or directions to transform the present into a future. An 'untimely' philosophy uses the history of philosophy, science and art as a toolbox. We should not seek to uncover what a philosophy or text *means*. We should look at what the philosophy *does*, or how it transforms the problems that in turn transform our thinking.

Deleuze's affirmation of his own philosophy as untimely relied to a certain extent on the destruction of what he saw as a dogma of Western thought that reached its zenith in modern capitalism. We tend, due to the very flow of life, to only perceive what concerns us. We abstract from becoming and see the world in terms of fixed 'territories'. We can then deterritorialise, to a certain extent, by imagining other beings through the images we have fixed, but we resist 'absolute deterritorialisation' or the total free play of images. It is in capitalism, though, that we take one fixed territory – the unit of capital – and imagine all possible beings or deterritorialisations as measured through capital. We see all life as homogeneous matter, there to be exchanged. Even concepts become 'information' to be marketed. Think of the way we 'sell' happiness, spirit or selfhood through brand names, therapy industries and advertising slogans. Being untimely, for Deleuze, meant being more than anti-capitalist. It meant disrupting the force that had allowed capitalism to emerge: the tendency to sameness, uniform quantification, the fixing of all becomings through one measure or 'territory' (of capital). Capitalism is only possible because we *can* reduce the complexity and difference of life to a single system of exchange. In capitalism it no longer matters *what* circulates – whether it is money, goods, information, or even the feel-good messages of feminism, multiculturalism and community – as long as there is constant exchange. For Deleuze this has a positive and negative side. Positively, it displays life's power of deterritorialisation: a capacity to take any actual thing and translate it into a movement of flow. We can take, for example, the images that once enslaved us – images of religion, law or authority – and see them as images, and we would do so by tearing them out of their origin and context. We can wander through galleries of religious art enjoying the intensity of paintings of hell and damnation, while not believing or being determined by their force. There is a positive capitalist tendency in all life, a deterritorialising tendency to open any system on to exchange and interaction. But deterritorialisation, which relies on an initial territorialisation, is also accompanied by reterritorialisation. Capital arrests its tendency to produce and open flows by quantifying all exchange through the flow of capital. In capitalism everything becomes measured by money or quantity – even the commodity value of art and the information value of concepts.

Being untimely for Deleuze did not mean looking back to a golden age before capitalism. Rather, one can only think 'out of joint' with one's time if we affirm the deterritorialising power of capital and the present beyond the present. This requires seeing life as a flow that is not the flow *of* some underlying substance (such as capital). Deleuze's 'context' was one in which everything had been placed in a context. Capitalism regards any age as an available commodity for the present: we watch historical dramas, wear 'retro' fashion, buy artefacts and heritage souvenirs and even include other cultures within the market as 'less developed' or 'earlier' versions of our own. As mentioned earlier in this book, the philosophy of Deleuze's day was phenomenology, in which all that is or becomes is seen as located within the life of consciousness. The dominant method of the social sciences of Deleuze's day was structuralism, in which any text or culture could be read and understood as a variation of an underlying and universal grammar or system. Deleuze's context was dominated and enclosed by the idea of context, the idea that difference is always difference within some common terrain. Deleuze's philosophy is anti-contextual. *Recognising* our culture, our discourses, or our 'construction of reality' is just one more way of allowing ourselves to remain who we are, enslaved to an 'image of thought'. Confronting inhuman, machinic or disconnected forces beyond our recognition is, for Deleuze, *active* thinking: a thinking that is not defined by an image it creates of itself, but that reforms itself over and over again, eternally.

This is perhaps the main reason to read Deleuze today, not because of his obvious relevance or resonance, but because of his *refusal* of who we are. In an age of 'multiculturalism' where it is asserted that we are all human and the same deep-down, Deleuze insisted that the human was an imposed image that imprisoned us, the most racist of all images. For it is racism that can only accept difference if it has already been tamed and recuperated by the same. In an epoch where we accept that each epoch has its own relative 'way of seeing' or thinking, Deleuze insisted on thinking the very powers of seeing and thinking, above and beyond any given culture or actual form. In an age where we believe that language structures our reality Deleuze argued that the 'real' included but went beyond events such as language; there are signs in nature and in inhuman life. In an age where we believe that art is just what institutions or galleries define as art, Deleuze insisted on the force of art as affect and the eternally new. In an age of communication, information and exchange, Deleuze insisted on the philosophical creation of concepts — concepts that resisted and complicated exchange and recognition. In an era of capitalism, where any exchange is quantifiable and reinvested to produce further exchange, Deleuze insisted on an expenditure and excess: productions that are not for any foreseeable or calculable end but that produce the new as such.

SUMMARY

Time is a process of differential becoming that constantly produces new events. We can think of this through the concept of the machine; life is a process of connections and proliferations with no ground, end or single intent. Through the proliferation of machines and connections we can think events. An event is not located within time; an event is the creation of a new line of time. We do, however, tend to homogenise and ground time, by seeing one event – such as human life – as the origin of all time and events. If we allow any one event to act as a foundation then we have subordinated the *active* force of time to one of its effects. This is the error of reactivism: enslaving the power of life, separating life from what it can do, from its future. Only the doctrine of eternal return can live up to the active challenge of life. The only true repetition is the repetition of difference, eternally reaffirming the creative difference of life. Philosophy and art are powers of the eternal only if they retake the challenge of difference with each new act of thinking. They promise absolute deterritorialisation: not just the freedom *from* this or that dogma or image, but the free flow and infinite creation of images. Capitalism is the historical epoch that is both most open and most closed to deterritorialisation. Capitalism seems to encourage the proliferation of the new, but this is always a new grounded on the principle of exchange.

4

TRANSCENDENTAL
EMPIRICISM

In this chapter we will look at Deleuze's explicit description of his own philosophy as 'transcendental empiricism', a term he used in his earlier work (*Difference and Repetition*, published in French in 1968) right up until *What is Philosophy?*, his much later work with Guattari. The main point is that Deleuze did not see transcendental empiricism as a theory; it was a challenge. Most *transcendental* philosophies have some sort of transcendental foundation that explains experience, the most usual being the 'subject'. But Deleuze constantly seeks freedom from any single ground or origin, precisely because he strives to think life as becoming rather than being. Transcendental *empiricism* therefore uses the concept of 'empiricism' – the concept of experience or givenness – to think of an experience, life or becoming that has no ground outside itself. Just as, in the last few chapters, we have seen how Deleuze tries to think time, machines and affects beyond the located point of human observers, so in his work on transcendental empiricism he tries to create an inhuman philosophy.

ART AND PHILOSOPHY

Philosophy forms concepts for our time that transform time. Art pulls experience apart to create percepts and affects that are not yet synthesised within a line of time. Deleuze's concept of the cinematic time-image is an act of philosophy in response to a particular event of art. The concept allows us to see cinema differently; we can go to the cinema and do more than follow the narrative and identify with the characters. We can allow cinema to engage us and transform us. The time-image, which will impose an incongruous sound over a discordant visual image and will then cut from image to image and voice to voice, undoes the single horizon of time from which 'we' view the world. We see time as a whole of diverging series and flows. If philosophy allows us to see cinema in this way (and therefore brings cinema to its own inner fulfilment), cinema also affects philosophy. Philosophy, for Deleuze, is not a 'theory' or explanation of the world. Like all thinking, philosophy is a 'heterogenesis' (Deleuze and Guattari 1994: 199). It is not just a becoming (genesis) but a becoming-other (hetero), and it does so in response to an other (chaos). Neither art nor philosophy are chaotic, but they would be nothing more than mere *opinions* if they did not allow an element of chaos to enter in and transform and mobilise thinking (Deleuze and Guattari 1994: 204).

The destruction of opinion is achieved by disrupting the supposed harmony or unity of experience. We need art to confront sensible singularities and philosophy to create unfounded concepts. The time-image, as a concept, works towards this end. On the one hand it asks us to see and create a cinema of irrational cuts and 'percepts' that are not attached to located observers. So cinema would become a new experience of the sensible, freeing perception from point of view and judgement. On the other hand, the *concept* of the time-image refers to the unseen or virtual power of difference from which any single percept emerges. (There can only be the singularity of the colour-image, for example, if there is the difference of light-waves, and then difference *as such*. It is the concept that *thinks*, but does not experience directly, this virtual power.) The concept does not just explain cinema; it takes the experience of affect in cinema and then allows us to *think* differently and in new directions, towards the flow of time itself. Art is sensory becoming, freeing us from ourselves to follow matter, while philosophy is conceptual becoming, recreating ourselves and what it is to think:

> By means of the material, the aim of art is to wrest the percept from perceptions of objects and the states of a perceiving subject, to wrest the affect from affections as the transition from one state to another: to extract a bloc of sensations, a pure being of sensations.
>
> (Deleuze and Guattari 1994: 167)

The task of philosophy when it creates concepts, entities, is always to extract an event from things and beings, always to give them a new event: space, time, matter, thought, the possible as events.

(Deleuze and Guattari 1994: 33)

TRANSCENDENCE

Deleuze's near contemporary and the subject of one of Deleuze's philosophical studies, Michel Foucault (1926–84), described the tradition of Western thought from which he was trying to break free as a 'subjection to transcendence' (Foucault 1972: 203). Transcendence (which is quite different from the transcendental) is that which transcends or lies outside. For Foucault, our thinking and institutions had always relied on some 'exteriority': something that we feel we can know, reveal or interpret and which will give us a foundation. Foucault argued that this resulted in an 'ethics of knowledge' whereby we imagine that if we get the facts about some outside world right then we will know what to do. In his book on Foucault, in his early work on philosophy and in his final co-authored work with the psychoanalyst Guattari, Deleuze laid out a path beyond transcendence. In contrast to transcendence as an 'ethics of knowledge' where we seek to obey some ultimate truth, Deleuze described his own philosophy as an ethics of *amor fati*: as love of *what is* (and not as the search for some truth, justification or foundation beyond, outside or transcendent to what is) (Deleuze 1990: 149). Part of this process of affirming 'what is' meant that philosophy had to be more than critical. It was not enough to expose the illusions of transcendence, not enough to show that all our invented foundations – such as God, Being or Truth – were inventions rather than givens. We also need to see the positive side of this inventive process. What is thinking such that it can enslave itself to images of some great outside? Does this not tell us that there is something productive, positive and liberating about the very power of thought?

The most obvious and general form of transcendence (and the one described by Foucault) is truth. Instead of seeing what we say and do as productive of relations between ourselves and our world, we imagine that there *is* some meaning or truth awaiting interpretation, revelation or disclosure. (This is the disease described by Deleuze and Guattari (1987) as 'interpretosis'.) It is this invention of truth that produces 'priests' (those who will lead us to the truth) and 'asceticism' (for we renounce our desires and enslave ourselves to supposedly higher ideals). More importantly, this whole process leads to nihilism: despair when that higher, truer world that we imagined behind appearances turns out to be ungraspable. In addition to truth, both Deleuze and Foucault described other more historically specific illusions of transcendence. Deleuze and Guattari describe the history of philosophy as the construction of 'planes of transcendence' whereby we create some foundation or ground for our thinking (Deleuze and Guattari 1994). We can see how the image of an external judging God whose law we need only reveal can provide thought with such a foundation, but so can less obvious notions like being, nature or culture. They all provide a plane within which all acts of thought and life can be explained. Deleuze cites even less obvious, more complex and far more relevant instances of transcendence. Perhaps the most important is the notion of the 'subject'. It is when we consider this example that we see how difficult it might be to think beyond transcendence. But it also helps to explain why Deleuze felt it necessary to press philosophy and art into pulling the supposed unified ground of experience apart into affects and concepts.

SUBJECTIVITY

The subject is a modern concept in philosophy which follows on from the 'death of God'. If we no longer assume that there is some divine power giving meaning and order to the world, then we have to explain how our world presents itself as a lawful and ordered unity. The explanation from the seventeenth-century philosopher, René Descartes (1596–1650), to the twentieth-century movement of phenomenology which Deleuze frequently criticises, is that experience is always given *to* a subject. Subjectivity is established by arguing that any truth, being or world that we know is an experienced world; everything is therefore open to doubt or question except for what is immediately experienced. What cannot be doubted or what remains beyond question is the subject, the one *who* experiences or doubts. This is expressed in Descartes' famous 'cogito': 'I think, therefore I am'. In doubting everything I am still thinking, and so there is some ground for certainty: the subject who thinks. Now this might seem to be a destruction of all 'transcendent' foundations and a restriction to nothing more than experience. Certainly, most twentieth- and twenty-first-century theory accepts this principle of the subject, a principle that according to Deleuze extends well beyond philosophy into popular culture and everyday life. We regard the world as there to be experienced by separate and observing subjects, even if we think of subjects as determined by culture, class or gender. It is a commonplace to see the world as 'subjectively' constructed, as dependent on human culture or language. For Deleuze, though, the subject is just one more form of transcendence (Deleuze 1990: 106). We may no longer have external foundations (such as God or the Truth) but we have created an 'image of thought' (Deleuze 1994: 131) that we accept as some ultimate foundation. This is what produces opinion and common sense, which takes the form of 'Everybody thinks that . . .' or 'We all know that . . .' or 'It would be mad or absurd to think that . . .' (Deleuze 1994). This is why art and philosophy are important. Not only do they invent forms of experience that are *not* those of some universally recognised subject, they also destroy the harmony of any single subject such that thinking is shattered into affects, concepts and observations.

In order to explain how the subject is constructed as a 'plane of transcendence' Deleuze describes the formation of the 'cogito' as a philosophical concept. *Cogito* is the Latin term for 'I think'. Descartes had argued that whatever we doubt we must at least still be thinking, so thinking can act as the ultimate ground. This assumes that there are experiences and that these are given to one who thinks. It does not consider that the 'I think' might be one effect among others in a 'swarm' of experiences. To begin with, Deleuze says that a concept, such as the cogito, is always a response to a problem, and so he is already saying that concepts cannot be ultimate foundations. Concepts occur as part of the active flow of life. The concept of the cogito, for example, is formed in response to the problem: what can I know with certainty? And this problem has already, Deleuze argues, laid out certain relations. When I begin with the question, 'What can I know?', I have already differentiated an 'I' from a world that I *then* strive to know. I have assumed that the way I relate to the world is one of knowledge and judgement, that the world is there as a set of possible facts to be represented and that the 'I' who doubts is set over and against the world and is representative of any possible experiencing self. The drama that lays out the concept of the cogito has three features. First, it assumes a 'conceptual persona' (Deleuze and Guattari

1994). All philosophy does this; we would not have any concepts without a 'dialoguing' Socrates or a 'mad' Nietzsche. The conceptual persona is not the author but the figure presupposed by the concept. Could we have 'Romanticism' without the figure of the Byronic individual (who is not the historical Byron but a broad-brushed character)? The persona of the 'cogito' is the solitary and doubting Descartes. Second, the concept creates, connects or is 'intensive and ordinal' (Deleuze and Guattari 1994). By ordinal Deleuze and Guattari refer to the order created by a concept, and by intensive they refer to the affects that a concept links together. Concepts do not just label and link up points, they create priorities, orders and 'zones of intensity' such as the privilege accorded to abstracted knowing. Descartes' concept expresses an affinity with doubting, judging, and approaching the world as representable matter. The concept does not just list features that are already there (as in the cardinal and extensive), but creates and desires specific lines of approach (the ordinal and intensive): 'Here I am', 'What can I know?', 'Here is my doubt', 'Thinking is certainty'. Third, transcendence, or an outside to thinking, is *produced* through this drama. We might say that there just 'is' experience, without subjects or objects, inside or outside. This is a plane of immanence, a pure flow of life and perception without any distinct perceivers. Deleuze refers to a 'plane of immanence' which is the presupposed field across which the distinction between interior (mind or subject) and exterior (world or certainty) is drawn. It is from experience that subjects are formed. There is perception, and it is from this perception that a perceiver is formed. This perceiver can then go on to form an image of itself as an 'I' in relation to some outside or transcendent world. Any truth or transcendence, any foundation or ground for experience, is always an event of experience. We do not begin as subjects who then have to know a world; there is experience and from this experience we form an image of ourselves as distinct subjects. Before 'the' subject of mind, then, there are what Deleuze refers to as 'larval subjects': a multiplicity of perceptions and contemplations not yet organised into a self. The notion of an outside or 'transcendent' world is produced from this immanence, not produced *by* a subject, but effected passively.

Deleuze therefore makes a distinction between 'exteriority' and the 'outside', and he does this most explicitly in his book on Foucault, *Foucault* (1988b; published in French in 1986), although the problem of immanence and the liberation from various forms of transcendence is a constant throughout his work. Thought creates 'planes of transcendence' which produce an exterior – such as the world we know, doubt or represent – and an interior – such as mind or the doubting subject. But this relation between interior and exterior relies on what remains hidden, presupposed or 'outside' rather than exterior. A door, for example, can create a border between interior or exterior, but this distinction would have to take place in space, which would be the more radical outside. Or, a piece of ribbon or paper might be folded to create a distinction between an inside and outside. But this division would rely on the paper itself which would be neither inside nor outside in a simple sense; the paper would be 'outside' the relation of interior and exterior produced by the fold. In the case of the subject, the inside of subjectivity and the exteriority of the world are produced from the radical outside of impersonal experience or perception. The 'outside' of thought, for Deleuze, is not what we know or represent; it is the 'plane of immanence', or all the assumptions, distinctions and distributions from which we think. Two things need to be noted here. First, this creation of transcendence from immanence extends well beyond philosophy. We can think of all life as a series of 'foldings', with each cell or organism being produced by creating an interior and exterior from the flow or milieu of life. Second, we need to see the positive or affirmative dimension of the history of thought as the construction of planes of transcendence. What inventive animals we must be to have constructed the transcendence of 'Truth', 'God', 'Being' or 'Eternity'.

Deleuze therefore suggests two responses to the illusion of transcendence in its philosophical and socio-political forms. The first is to affirm transcendence as an event or creation, to see that any ground, origin or ultimate outside is effected from experience. This is one of the reasons to do history and history of philosophy, to look at all the diverse planes or grounds that we have produced. Deleuze and Guattari's *A Thousand Plateaus*, as the title suggests, looks at a history of planes or plateaus upon which life appears to be grounded: language seems to presuppose the speaking subject; genetic mutation seems to be grounded on species; various social systems appear to be produced from 'men'; and all our economic relations suggest that there is some primary material that is there to be exchanged. But these explanatory grounds, planes or plateaus are *not* original or ultimate conditions which can be used to explain life. The ground is an effect of production; life articulates itself in two directions, producing ground and grounded. From the immanence of life distinct forms or strata are differentiated. There is a general flow, for example, of genetic variation. But the illusion of transcendence begins from formed organisms and then sees variation as grounded on species. The error of transcendence mistakenly reverses the relation between difference and identity. We think of difference and variation as grounded upon identity, rather than points of identity being abstracted from difference. We think of genetics as leading up to man, rather than man being an event within a flow of genetic variation. We think of language as a 'tool' for speakers, rather than as a differential force that produces speaking positions.

IMMANENCE

If the first response to the illusion of transcendence is to think all the different grounds, origins and foundations which have operated as 'planes of transcendence', the second and far less easily achieved task is to think 'THE plane of immanence' as such (Deleuze and Guattari 1994: 59). We can go back to Deleuze's work on cinema to draw a parallel. Cinema is the linking of images and the imaging of movements; but at its height cinema can present not just this or that image but the very flow or connection from which any image is differentiated. In so doing we move from the actual – a given image or sequence – to the virtual – the event of temporal flow above and beyond any of its produced forms.

The two works in which Deleuze and Guattari confront the plane of immanence most explicitly are *What is Philosophy?* (where they theorise the plane of immanence) and *A Thousand Plateaus* where they actively explore all the genetic, geological, microbiological, historical and aesthetic becomings from which thinking emerges. For this reason, *A Thousand Plateaus* does not take the conventional form of a book and argument; it has no distinct beginning and seems to capture immanence itself – with each plateau (or chapter) being as good an entry point to the exploration as any other. Thinking 'THE plane of immanence' requires a distinction into three levels or planes, but each plane already implies and opens out to its other. First, there is chaos or the flows of difference that are life, prior to any organised matter or system of relations. Deleuze and Guattari refer to this as the 'chaosmos'. It is not yet a 'world'; nor is it life perceived as a whole (cosmos) formed out of chaos; it is radically outside. Second, from this flow of difference or these singular forces and intensities certain organisms are differentiated. And each organism forms a point of perception or opens out in two directions: towards the chaos from which it emerges and to its own limited form. Each species for example has an element of constancy and variation. The human organism opens out to chaos by imagining the ground from which it emerges, but it always does so from the recognisable position of the human. Deleuze and Guattari refer to this as 'double articulation'. Life does not produce closed forms, but 'strata' – relatively stable points that slow the flow of difference down by creating a distinction between inside and outside. We could think of this second level as the creation of transcendence or 'world' from the immanent flow of life; and each organism has its own opening to the world. Finally, philosophy or thinking *the* plane of immanence is never chaos itself, never a full return to the first level of 'absolute deterritorialisation'. Philosophy, Deleuze and Guattari argue, 'gives consistency' to chaos, allows us to think the immanent difference which has produced transcendence. The plane of immanence, as thought by philosophy, is not the ground or foundation of life; the plane of immanence is the thought of that which produces any ground. In the case of the 'cogito' or subject, for example, which is produced as a ground, Deleuze and Guattari argue that there is a presupposed plane of immanence: relations of doubt, knowledge, certainty, matter and thinking. The plane of immanence is the outside or 'prephilosophical' element in any philosophy. Thinking *the* plane of immanence means thinking of this outside in general, this power of difference or distribution which allows activities, such as art and philosophy, not just to perceive a world but to think the very difference from which any world emerges.

The task of thinking immanence can take a number of forms and has to be renewed over and over again. Artists must constantly plunge back into the depths of experience in order to release the sensibilities from which actual experience is composed. Philosophers have to recreate concepts that give 'consistency' to chaos; we have to constantly reopen thinking to the outside without allowing a fixed image of that outside to act as one more foundation. Philosophers create concepts that, far from functioning as grounds or points of agreement and recognition, allow us to think of the difference, discontinuity and chaos which surrounds and passes through us.

Deleuze comes up with a number of such concepts as well as citing a number of previous philosophers who have also affirmed immanence. Baruch de Spinoza (1632–77), for example, refused to see God as some external being who created a separate world. If we thought of God as outside creation then there would be something other than God, and God would not be absolute. For Spinoza, therefore, God is nothing other than expressive substance, and substance is nothing other than its expression. There is not a substance that then expresses itself in different ways. There are just differences of expression, with no expression lying outside or grounding any other. For Spinoza it is only our limited ideas that have us see the world as grounded on distinct and separate substances; our limited imagination thinks of God as a father figure in the heavens. Adequate ideas would see all life in terms of the one absolute expression which has no ground outside itself; God would not be a separate and concrete personification but an infinite power that *is* all life. Adequate ideas, therefore, free us from the limits of our imagination and ask us to think beyond ourselves. For this reason – and Deleuze insists on this dimension of Spinoza – philosophy would be active and practical: expanding our ideas of a world of already differentiated terms to think the expressive power which produces those terms. Immanence for Deleuze is a task with a futural dimension.

We need to create ways of thinking which do not allow for the production of a transcendent image that will enclose and explain experience. For this reason Deleuze constantly created new concepts and new vocabularies, and even combined competing viewpoints in the same work, such as the multiple voices of *A Thousand Plateaus*. Such a proliferation of voices, concepts and viewpoints precludes us from thinking that the whole of life can be comprehended. At the same time, though, while the whole of life is beyond any actual perception we have of it, this does not mean that thought cannot confront and transform itself by striving to think this whole. Deleuze's own works and concepts are a case in point: his creation of difficult, unconventional and revolutionary texts has changed the way we view ourselves. We are no longer privileged subjects who view life in disengaged theoretical contemplation; through Deleuze we can start to question who we are and what we might become. Thinking experience as an open and immanent whole acknowledges that each new event of experience will transform what experience *is,* thereby precluding in principle any final or closed ground for experience. Immanence is, then, for Deleuze the only true philosophy. If we allow thought to accept some transcendent foundation – such as reason, God, truth or human nature – then we have stopped thinking. And if immanence is philosophy for Deleuze it is also an ethics: not allowing experience to be enslaved by any single image that would elevate itself above others.

All along here, in defining immanence, we have been referring to experience – arguing that we cannot use an image to ground experience. But what do we mean by experience here and what stops experience from acting as one more (transcendent) ground? This brings us to Deleuze's empiricism and once again, to the necessary intersection and difference of philosophy and art.

EMPIRICISM

Empiricism is, for Deleuze, more than a philosophical theory or commitment to a particular school of thought. It is an ethics and a politics. Traditionally, empiricism is defined in contrast with idealism. Idealism argues for the primacy of ideas. For an idealist, the only way in which we have a world or experience is if certain fundamental ideas can organise or constitute a world. Without the ideas of causality or substance, for example, the data we receive or intuit would just be a random chaotic influx. We only have a *world* because what we receive – experience or the given – is mediated or organised by ideas. Idealism is, therefore, also a commitment to some notion of a subject who orders or constitutes their world *as a world.* Now, idealism may seem to be a specific branch of philosophy but it is far more than this. Today, in literary theory and cultural studies we often think of the world as 'constructed' through language or culture. Even more generally, when we refer to the world we refer to *the* shared human world that we know. We do not think of plants, molecules or machines as having a world precisely because we only refer to a world if it is conceptualised or represented in ideas. Do animals have a world? A dog may, but does a goldfish or a beetle? For an idealist it all depends on whether there is not just data, but data that forms some meaningful perceived whole. There is a privilege accorded to consciousness, or experience that is recognised and reflected. Idealism acknowledges that there is a life and a real world outside our ideas, but it insists that this life or 'real' is *mediated* or conditioned by ideas. The real is always a real given through ideas. Deleuze argues against mediation. He insists that it is not the case that there is a life or being which is then mediated or ordered by ideas; life is lived directly and immediately. We do not perceive a picture or idea of the sun, we experience sunlight itself. Indeed, far from our ideas *ordering* our world; the world itself produces ideas – or images – of which we are effects.

Empiricism, in contrast with idealism, argues that ideas do not order experience; ideas are the *effect* of experience. There is no condition outside the world – such as the subject – that allows the world to be given. Empiricism commits itself to conditions that are no greater than what is given and conditioned. Put more concretely, we cannot use the subject and his ideas to *explain* the world or experience; we have to account for how the subject is formed *from experience*. An idealist would argue that we have a causally ordered world because 'we' connect experiences into a sequence, *through the idea of causality*.

An empiricist argues that there is an experience of sequence – such as 'a' following 'b' – and that this sequence *eventually produces the idea of causality*. Ideas are reflections of experience, formed from experience. The subject is not the author of these ideas. Rather, experience takes place in the mind, and from a series of experiences a subject is formed. The mind is nothing more than the 'site' where experience takes place (and we need to remember that there are other sites, such as non-mental experiences). The mind receives the impression of 'a' then 'b'. It connects or synthesises these impressions or images, but the point for Deleuze is that there is no subject *who* connects. Rather, there is connection and the mind is nothing more than the site where connection takes place.

The next stage or level is the more interesting one. There is a connection of 'a' then 'b', allowed by the flow of time; this is then repeated, precisely because it is the nature of life to produce over and over again. At some point the mind not only registers 'a' then 'b', it anticipates or expects 'b'. We expect the sun to rise, we anticipate that our neighbour will say hello, or we expect that other societies will be much like our own; these expectations and anticipations *produce* a cause: such as the idea of a law of nature that causes the sun to rise or a law of human nature that produces us all as the same. In the expectation the mind forms the idea of a cause, and mind is nothing more than a power of connections. By expecting an event the mind has gone beyond experience (or the given) towards the future, and has done so by relating the present to the past. The crucial point is this: that this imagination which produces ideas begins *from within life*, as part of life's creative flow. Ideas are products of the imagination. But the ideas that go beyond experience nevertheless *extend* experience; they do not organise or construct experience from some separate subjective (or ideal) point of view.

This may seem all very abstract but it has two crucial political implications. First, we can no longer think of experience as experience *of* some subject. The impersonal, inhuman or anonymous plane of experience goes well beyond knowledge and the human world. There are all sorts of experiences and perceptions or impressions: plants perceiving light, the muscles of the body experiencing strain, genes experiencing viral mutation. The human subject is the effect of one particular series of experiential connections. From material impressions – sense data that are received by the body – the mind forms *incorporeal* ideas: the expectation of a future, the idea of a general human experience, the idea of a 'self' and the idea of a lawful and ordered world. Experience is not confined to human experience, which means that there is a multiplicity of *worlds*. We need to expand the notion of experience to include all the different events of response and impression that characterise life. This includes the body's affects – before being ordered and represented by ideas – and affects beyond the human. There are molecular perceptions and non-organic lines of difference. The human subject is an effect of all these diverse becomings, all the molecular, genetic, bodily and incorporeal connections which traverse any organism.

EMPIRICISM AND ASSEMBLAGES

The second consequence of Deleuze's empiricism is more directly pertinent to literary theory. Ideas are formed by extending lines of experience; from a series of experiences of 'a' following 'b' the mind that contemplates the series can expect 'a' to follow 'b'. The subject is therefore constituted within the given or experience but also imagines or projects to the not-yet given future. Social institutions or 'social machines' as Deleuze and Guattari describe them, are *collective* extensions or 'assemblages' that extend experience. Imagine, for example, a body that connects with another body and in this connection draws off pleasure. Deleuze and Guattari refer to these connections of bodies as 'desiring machines' and they do so according to a strict empiricism. We should begin from experiences or perceptions without *grounding* those experiences in some privileged site such as the subject. Desiring machines are, accordingly, nothing more than their connections or experiences. From the connections of bodies or from experience, human minds form ideas. The child's mouth, for example, that has experienced pleasure at the breast comes to desire or anticipate the breast. In this expectation desire can produce an image or 'investment'. This is what Deleuze means when he says that desire is productive. We often think that desire is for what we lack, but for Deleuze desire is *more* than the actual. In the case of the child, the mouth's past pleasure produces an idea or image of further pleasure, and this creates an 'investment'. The breast becomes more than what it actually is (a body part) and takes on an added virtual dimension – the breast of fantasy, pleasure and desire. Social machines extend and organise these 'partial' investments into organised institutions, such as 'motherhood', 'the family' or 'culture'. It is the capacity for *imagination* to expect, anticipate or extend experience that produces formations that *seem* to govern human life but which are actually outgrowths or 'fictions' produced from life.

Empiricism is a commitment to beginning from singular, partial or 'molecular' experiences, which are then organised and extended into 'molar' formations. (In *Anti-Oedipus* Deleuze and Guattari describe their approach both as a molecular politics – composed from partial objects – and a 'schizoanalysis', which breaks up larger social forms into their singular parts.) Before there is a 'child' who relates to a 'mother' – before there are these social selves – there is a pre-personal perception, the connection of mouth and breast. Ideas, sense or the imagination extend these impersonal connections of matter. Ideas have a singular and inhuman beginning. We only have the idea of the 'human' or the 'subject' *after* bodies connect to form regular sequences and *then* reflect and expand these sequences into some general notion of 'subjectivity'.

For Deleuze, empiricism is an ethics precisely because it takes any social formation, even one as general as 'humanism' and shows its emergence. We do not begin *from* an idea, such as human culture, and then use that idea to explain life. We chart the emergence of the idea from particular bodies and connections. We can see how this might open up new ways for thinking about literature. There are two ways that we can think about literary character. The first is to say that there is a general human form which novelists then describe in its varying forms, adding nuances and particulars. The history of literature would then *represent* the vast array of human life. And we could see novels as representative of this human life or at least of the modern self. Certainly, many literary forms are produced in this way – as if there were some human template upon which distinct experiences could be played out. At the extreme we might call to mind the lowest quality soap operas, where characters are pretty much the same, differentiated by no more than their physical appearance and a simple moral divide between good and evil. There is a bland and shared humanness, where everyone can fall in and out of love with anyone else. The only disruptions come from marked villains; every soap has its 'bitch' or 'bastard' who exists outside the norm of agreeable humanity. On the other hand, and at the other extreme, we could begin from *affect*, diverse experiences that have no prior ground and that go to make up characters who are incongruous collections of 'intensities'. Deleuze cites the fiction of the French novelist Marcel Proust (1871–1922), on whom he wrote a book-length study in 1964 (Deleuze 1973), where the beloved becomes a whole 'world' of gestures, textures, smells and memories, all of which open a whole new and hidden line of becoming, thoroughly beyond recognition. But even the novels of Charles Dickens can give us a sense of the human as the production *of life and difference*, and not as the ground from which life is perceived. Dickens composes characters from quirky phrases, strange body tics, irrational desires and affections and highly partial histories. Character is not a single unified ground or body which then has certain distinguishing features; characters are collections or 'assemblages' of randomly gathered affects. Miss Haversham in *Great Expectations* is a hatred of men, a rotting wedding cake, a decaying body, a memory of loss, a darkened room and a desire for revenge. Characters are the diverse events and histories that compose them, and the same applies to any self. We are nothing more than our contracted habits and contemplations; we are events *of life* – and a life that is nothing outside all these singular expressions. The other person is not just like us, with a few character differences. The other is another possible world of differences. Literature, if it is worthy of the name, is not the *representation* of a human life that we all share and recognise; it is the creation of affects that open other worlds. In the case of the novel these affects are opened up from the possible world of another character.

LITERATURE AND EMPIRICISM

Deleuze's empiricism implicitly and explicitly makes a clear distinction between what is *really* literature and what merely circulates as banal popular culture. For Deleuze, literature is not the repetition of already formed generalities. The Mills and Boon romance that I read to confirm the sense and possibility of true love and whose female heroine I recognise as 'just like me' is *not* literature. Such supposedly literary forms begin from already assumed ideas – the timelessness of love and the norms of human desire. True literature begins from diverse affects or experiences and traces their organisation into characters or persons. It is not surprising that Deleuze often mentioned Virginia Woolf (1882–1941) and other modernist authors, whose stream of consciousness technique presented a highly specific flow of experience that runs through consciousness, producing and effecting characters, rather than being grounded in characters. But we do not need to go this far, and we can think of the consequences of empiricism in relation to other styles.

We *could* read Jane Austen's novels, for example, as representations of *the* drama of human love and marriage and thereby explain the contemporary appeal of her work (as well as all the film adaptations). Alternatively, we could take our cue from immanence and empiricism. We could see her novels as a diagnosis or symptomatology of social forms, such that social norms are traced from specific desires or investments. Unlike the Mills and Boon romance, Austen does not assume the idea of marriage as a transcendent good; she shows how that idea or social institution is imagined, produced and sustained. Austen shows how certain affects produce the masculine, the feminine and their order in marriage. (The sustained appeal of her work would tell us that this organisation of affect is still in operation today.) Austen's characters all begin with diverse desires and investments. In *Pride and Prejudice* the daughters are differentiated by quirky character marks – a love of books and music, an almost dogmatic commitment to moral arguments, an investment in military costumes and the accompanying masculine rituals, the desire for marriage of whatever kind, giggling, gossip and fashion. Each character is a composite of these affects which all have a clear social or collective investment: fashion, gossip and frivolity function as 'signs' of the feminine. But Austen's novels always show how the feminine is coded from some of these affects and not others. Certain affects and qualities have a wide social circulation; fashion and gossip are repeated, emphasised and seem to form the very 'whole' of any female life. Other affects are displayed by Austen as female – for they make up so many of her characters – but nevertheless out of step with the social machine. In *Pride and Prejudice* the central narrative marriage almost fails to take place because of the overly moral and judgemental character of the heroine. The female affects of learning, morality, music and judgement are not socially recognised. Austen's novels both show how affects make up various characters, and then show how those affects are organised by social wholes. Marriage only includes females formed from certain affects, and excludes others. 'Marriage' is displayed as an institution formed from irrational ideas and restricted imaginings. All these character 'refrains' in Austen's novels do not, like the easy romance, hurtle towards the destiny of marriage. Austen's characters seem to be 'squeezed' into the institution of marriage. Marriage takes the minutiae and divergence of affects and gives it the general and recognisable form of the male/female or husband/wife couple. Novels like Austen's can be read as exercises in empiricism. They dissect the institutions – such as love, law and marriage – that seem to govern and organise life and show how these fictions are composed by the selection of certain affects. They show how characters are nothing more than the partial experiences that accrue from within life, even if there are institutions such as marriage that will recognise us all as equally and homogeneously human.

Literature opens up two sides of empiricism. On the one hand it presents the affects that go to make up larger forms. There is a critical strand in Austen, for example, which displays how the feminine has been assembled from frivolity, sensualism, mindlessness and false ideas of romance. On the other hand, literature goes beyond the presentation of diverse affects to the positive organisation of those affects into ideas. Fiction and imagination is part of the very production of life. We produce ideas of the self, of society and of institutions such as justice or democracy. In its legitimate form such productions are immanent; we recognise them as produced fictions for the sake of life. In its illegitimate form such productions become transcendent; we think we should obey or recognise the idea of society, justice or democracy, which supposedly governs our experience. Literature is one of the sites in which such ideas can be displayed *as fictions*. 'Marriage' in Austen is assembled from economic, social and affective lines of experience. There is a legitimate and immanent form of marriage in Austen, when two persons create their own alliance and marriage is used to enhance their power. But there is also an illegitimate and transcendent use, where the character is ruled by the idea of marriage as some imposed norm: marry at whatever cost, for the sake of the idea itself. Fiction is at the heart of empiricism because it exposes the productions and extensions of ideas from their affective components.

It is not by chance perhaps that love is such a dominant motif in novels, and in Deleuze's work on life and literature. In his work on Proust Deleuze had shown how the perception of the beloved opens up another world. Fiction helps us avert the illusion of transcendence. It is the error of transcendence to think that there is *a* world that we need to represent through a separate order of signs. For empiricism, all life is a flow of signs; each perception is a sign of what lies beyond, and there is no ultimate referent or 'signified' that lies behind this world of signs. (Deleuze's method here is opposed to structuralism, which argues that we produce a meaningful world or 'signified' through imposed systems of signs or 'signifiers'.) In love, and the fiction of love, the other or beloved, is the 'sign' of a whole world of affects and intensities that are not our own. If we accept the principle of empiricism – which is that there is that there is no principle that can order experience from outside – then there will be as many worlds as there are minds. Each point in experience opens up to the whole of the world but does so from its own specific becoming. Literature is the exploration of the diverse worlds of others and the novel, especially, presents love as an encounter between the divergent worlds of lover and beloved.

TRANSCENDENTAL EMPIRICISM

Empiricism is, then, a commitment to immanence. Any idea that we use to explain experience is itself an event within experience. The risk of empiricism, though, is that we locate this experience as immanent *to* some 'plane'. We tend to define experience as human experience, or consciousness or culture. We think of experience as what is present *to us*, as what is actual. We fail to realise that we are events within a much broader terrain of experience that extends well beyond what we actively know. The principle of immanence demands that we do not see experience as the experience *of* some being or some ultimate subject. Rather, there is a flow or multiplicity of experiences *from which* any being or idea is effected. Deleuze therefore qualified his particular form of empiricism as a 'radical empiricism', a 'superior empiricism' and a 'transcendental empiricism'. There had been a long history of empiricism, going back to the eighteenth-century Scottish philosopher David Hume, which argued that ideas were effects of experience (Deleuze 1991). However, experience had been taken as human or conscious experience, the experience *of* some experiencing being. A *transcendental* empiricism, by contrast, insists that there is no ground, subject or being *who* experiences, just experience. The cosmos, Deleuze and Guattari eventually argue, is a plane or 'planomenon' of intersecting flows of life, all propelled by difference (Deleuze and Guattari 1987). The light and heat that drives the prebiotic soup into the production of life, the mutation of a genetic chain because of the 'leap' of a virus, the sunflower that turns to the sun, or the orchid that becomes what it is only in the cross-fertilisation enabled by the wasp: all these are forms of perception or experience:

> Contemplating is creating, the mystery of passive creation, sensation. . . . The plant contemplates by contracting the elements from which it originates – light, carbon, and the salts – and it fills itself with colors and odors that in each case qualify its variety, its composition: it is sensation in itself.
>
> (Deleuze and Guattari 1994: 212)

Transcendental empiricism frees thought of any ultimate metaphysical foundation by insisting that far from being some actual ground, life is a virtual multiplicity, not of things and agents but contemplations and contractions, events and responses. It is not that there are persons or beings who then contemplate the world; there are contemplations that are passive and impersonal. These contemplations create distinct human bodies and organisms.

This means that there is not a world (actual) that is *then* represented in images (virtual) by the privileged mind of man (the subject). Life is just this actual–virtual interaction of imaging: each flow of life becomes other in response to what it is not. The anticipation goes beyond what is actual, but also produces a new actual. The image is neither actual nor virtual but the interval that brings actuality out of the virtual. The plant 'images' or perceives the sun towards which it turns, allowing for the becoming of photosynthesis; and what it *is* to be a plant is nothing more than this becoming, experiencing or imaging:

> There are images, things are themselves images, because images aren't in our brain. The brain's just one image among others. Images are constantly acting and reacting on each other, producing and consuming. There's no difference at all between *images, things*, and motion.
>
> (Deleuze 1995: 42)

This refusal to see images or becoming as housed within a privileged image (such as the brain), this refusal to attribute experience to an observer or subject, makes experience transcendental. It allows experience to act as a transcendental principle: a principle that does not set itself up outside the given in some grand position of detached judgement. The error of thought or its fundamental illusion is *transcendence*, where we begin from some already given term or foundation that acts as an outside or ground for our arguments. A *transcendental* approach, on the other hand, asks how any outside or any given term is produced; it therefore leads us into, not away from, experience. How, for example, did we come to experience mind or man as the ground of the world? It is *transcendent* to say that all life begins from human experience or subjectivity, because in such a case we have presupposed the subject. It is *transcendental* to show how the subject is produced as an effect. There are experiences; these are connected to form images of bodies; the body that *contemplates* those connections mistakenly sees itself as the author or ground of those connections. This is the illusion of the transcendent subject, the subject as plane within which experience takes place.

It might seem, then, that a transcendental approach would amount to the destruction of all those ideas and images that are produced from experience but then come to enslave experience. If we start to feel a duty towards man, a desperate demand to find ourselves, or an imperative to live up to the idea of humanity, then we have taken an image from experience and used it to legislate over experience. (In his book on Nietzsche, *Nietzsche and Philosophy*, published in French in 1962, Deleuze remarks that 'consciousness' is always that of the slave, for the very idea of consciousness fixes the flow of experience into a being; we start to *recognise* an image of ourselves, rather than allowing further creation (Deleuze 1983).) As a philosophical method transcendentalism has direct political implications. If we cannot begin from any founding (or transcendent) term, then *nothing* – neither justice, nor democracy, nor law, nor humanity – can be appealed to as a ground for political arguments. (Deleuze and Guattari's lever in political arguments always invokes a 'people to come': not the fulfilment of an idea, but the production or becoming of future ideas.) This would seem to leave us with the notion that all Deleuze's transcendental empiricism can do is to destroy illusory ideas, and all literature can do would be to make life more chaotic by multiplying affects and intensities beyond organising ideas. There is, however, a positive side to Deleuze's transcendental method, and it lies in the alternative approach he offers to ideology. We will look at Deleuze's political theory and counterargument to ideology in the next chapter.

SUMMARY

Deleuze's philosophy is a transcendental empiricism. But this method is not just one method 'within philosophy'; it is based on the challenge of life. If we accept that all life is a flow of becoming and interaction (or 'experience' in its broadest possible sense), then philosophy will have to be a commitment to experience. Philosophy will be empiricism. Philosophy can only be a *transcendental* empiricism if it does not set up some foundation outside experience. Experience cannot be grounded on man, the subject, culture or language. There is just an immanent flow of experience from which distinct beings, such as human subjects, are formed. Western thought has tended to take one of these beings as the ground for all experience; this is the illusion of transcendence. Deleuze's method works against this dogma and strives to think experience well beyond its human and fixed images. This, he argues, is an ethical and practical task. It will free us from the restrictions of common sense and a moral image of human reason, allowing us to become towards the future. One way of thinking empiricism is to see all life as a flow and connection of interacting bodies, or 'desiring machines'. These connections form regularities, which can then be organised through 'social machines'. It is the task of philosophy and art to chart the ways in which bodies imagine and produce fictions, ideas or assemblages that *seem* to be transcendent but which are really produced from the very flow of life.

5

DESIRE, IDEOLOGY
AND SIMULACRA

Deleuze's entire project set itself against lack and negation. We have already seen how, from the camera to life as transcendental experience, he provides a positive definition of the image. Images are not pale replicas or second-rate versions of a real world. Images are fully real, from the images produced by a camera to the images produced by the eye that expects what lies beyond its immediate viewpoint. Desire, for Deleuze, is also positive and productive, and this allows for a radically new approach to politics and the relation between politics and the imagination. Desire does not begin from lack – desiring what we do not have. Desire begins from connection; life strives to preserve and enhance itself and does so by connecting with other desires. These connections and productions eventually form social wholes; when bodies connect with other bodies to enhance their power they eventually form communities or societies. Power is, therefore, not the repression of desire but the expansion of desire. Against the notion that social wholes are formed through ideology – some repressive idea to which we submit – Deleuze argues for social wholes as positive and productive. Social wholes take *desires* – or those connections which enhance life – in order to produce *interests* – 'coded', regular, collective and organised forms of desire. The mouth that connects with the breast produces and enhances life and desire, but the socially ordered image of this connection – as motherhood or the family – produces that local *desire* as a general *interest*. The problem of the usual explanation of social power is, for Deleuze, that it begins with interests: assuming that we come in to the world with ready-made ideas or desires *for* some specific end. The task of his own method is to explain how *interests* – such as humanism, individualism, capitalism or communism – are produced from *desires*: the concrete and specific connection of bodies.

IDEOLOGY

There has been a long history in literary and cultural theory that launches its criticism from the notion of ideology. The concept of ideology takes many complex forms but in general it explains how individuals act against their interests. Ideology, therefore, is seen as the production of an imaginary dimension that masks oppression. This can take the form of explicit propaganda: we are told that the market forces that exploit us are the only means to human freedom, and this can occur through overtly political messages. For literary criticism, though, ideology is usually seen in more complex forms. Literature gives form and reason to a world that might otherwise be recognised as exploitative. For example, women read romance novels and identify with the ideal of marriage; they then freely acquiesce to being passive pawns in the game of patriarchy. Ideology, then, is a way of explaining how economic or material exploitation is masked by images.

Deleuze's transcendental method is a form of critique quite different from ideology. Ideology has to assume that there are real interests that are concealed: that women, say, *really* want to be liberated but are duped by ideology. Ideology also has to assume some *normative* form of the individual who awaits liberation from the imposed illusions of culture. Such an approach has a negative concept of power and the imagination; power is what oppresses or distorts an otherwise 'real' world, and imagination is the faculty of delusion.

From a transcendental point of view, though, we cannot assume real interests, nor some pre-social and essential individual that we might discover underneath power and images. The first step of transcendental method for Deleuze is to show how persons and interests are produced from the chaotic flows of desire. Deleuze and Guattari refer to this as 'micropolitics'. It shows how the extended and individual categories of persons, classes or interests are 'coded' from affects. To return to the example of Jane Austen or any novelistic composition of character, we can see how the description of fabrics, skin colour, gestures, rhythms of speech and body-parts – the thinness of waist, the delicacy of frame – make up 'femininity'. It is not that there are women who are then *misrepresented* through ideological stereotypes. 'Woman' is an assemblage of socially coded affects, and literature at its best explores all the affects and intensities that have gone into making up the images of personhood. Deleuze and Guattari refer to micropolitics or 'schizoanalysis' as the art of seeing the composition of generalities from singular investments. Supposedly personal qualities, they argue, begin impersonally and politically. The feminine quality of being 'fair' (to go back to Austen) elevates whiteness, and is therefore already political in the sense of working with racial groupings of bodies. The masculine qualities of strength, courage and valour (again in Austen) have a military history. Today, we might think of femininity as exemplified (for some) in the image of Princess Diana. But this is not the imposition of a stereotype on women. It is the production of 'woman' from political affects. Diana is composed from whiteness, delicacy, good breeding and a charitable humanism. Before there are the private individuals of 'men' and 'women' there is a political coding of affects. The 'father', Deleuze and Guattari argue, is always also the banker, the cop, the tax man and the politician. The supposedly general forms of humanity, masculinity and femininity, are composed from political intensities.

A transcendental method does not begin from assumed terms, such as 'man' or 'human interests'; it shows the historical composition of those terms from intensities. This means, contra ideology, that desire is not *repressed* by politics so much as it is *coded*. A desire – say, the connection of male and female bodies – becomes an *interest* when it is coded as the sacred bourgeois marriage that, far from being the effect of our desire appears as a law that ought to govern our desire. Political formations or 'social machines' produce interests from desires. A group of bodies connect to expand their power; this is desire. That same group of bodies forms an image of themselves as the very ground of human life; this is interest. It is by this process that particular investments, such as the collection of bodies of a certain tribe, can be coded as a universal interest: the local investment in whiteness becomes a global investment in 'man'. Liberation, in Deleuze and Guattari's approach, cannot appeal to underlying interests, such as the emancipation of 'man', for man was always formed from specific and singular affects. Rather, they seek to release the impersonality of desires from interests. Theories of ideological politics work at a *cognitive* level and assume that we are being deceived or misled by power; peel away the power and images and there we will be. Deleuze's transcendental method refuses to posit a being outside power and imaging. *Desire itself is power, a power to become and produce images.* Desire also has the power to produce images that enslave it: images of a moral 'man' obeying his social duty. But the task is not to get away from images so much as to reveal and intensify their production: why limit ourselves to the image of man and woman as social citizens, why not *become other*? Deleuze's political critique does not begin from a power that opposes desire but from one single *univocal* flow of desire that produces the very terms that enslave it. Univocal, because no form of power is capable of grounding or explaining any other. Power does not oppress us; it produces us. Cultural forms, like literature, do not *deceive* us; they are ways in which desire organises and extends its investments. This can work positively, when intensities and affects are multiplied to produce further possibilities for experience. Think of modernist novels, such as Virginia Woolf's *The Waves* (1931), where affects and percepts flow across characters, with the 'narrative' often wandering undecidably from one character's point of view to another. Woolf's novel was radical, not just because it presented multiple viewpoints with no privileged centre, but because the viewpoints were nothing more than flows of experience. There were not characters *who perceived*, so much as sites of perception or 'blocks of becoming' which were vaguely identified with proper names. Data, sensations and perceptions seem to flow through characters, thus showing characters to be nothing more than the images they encounter, nothing more than their singular becoming. Alternatively, literature can work negatively and transcendently, where affects and intensities are read as signs or symbols of some underlying subject or human essence. Think of 'New Age' culture where our dreams, our bodily tics, our colouring and physical type are read as signifiers of who we are really, where all affect refers to the person lying in wait for a therapist's interpretation. Here, everything happens for a reason; everything is a 'signifier' of a self just waiting to be revealed.

UNIVOCITY AND PLURALISM

If we accept the transcendental principle that we cannot explain experience from any privileged point but need to begin from the flow of experience itself, then we will also have to accept that no *being* can be used to explain or order existence. There can be only one univocal plane of being. For Deleuze, univocity is a radical philosophical possibility that sets itself against transcendence. Transcendence is equivocal: positing a being that is – the outside world – and a being that knows or represents – mind or 'man'. Univocity posits one plane of becoming with no point being the ground or knower. We cannot begin from a material world known by intelligible mind and assume that mind is a separate type of being; this would be *equivocity* or the positing of more than one substance, more than one 'voice' of being. The problem with equivocity is logical and ethical. Logically, it makes no sense to say that there is being as matter on the one hand and being as mind on the other. Insofar as both of these things *are* then they express one common existence. Western thought has tended to set one type of being over and against the other, as the ground of the other. But in order to do so it must adopt a position in relation to these two types of being, both mind and matter. So mind and matter will always be *within* experience and cannot be used as distinct beings to explain experience. Ethically, the positing of two types of being has enabled a ground for morality; either mind gives ideas to the world or mind represents the order of the world. However, if there is only one plane of univocal being then no being can ground or speak for any other, all beings will be expressions of the one plane of being. Every distinct expression or becoming will be on a par with every other. The metaphysical tradition of the West has been predominantly dualist or equivocal, imagining that there is a moral hierarchy of more than one type of being: a God outside the world who truly *is*, with everything else existing by lesser degrees or by 'analogy'. Usually, equivocity takes the form of intelligible mind being elevated above sensible nature. For Deleuze, though, mind is one mode of becoming that expresses a life that undertakes a multiplicity of becomings. If there is no privileged being, if there is only one being, then we are also within a *pluralism*. Each expression of being becomes in its own way without reference or relation to any grounding being. No expression of being is in itself good or evil; there is no separate ordering principle for the world.

Values and relations (such as good and evil) are *selected* from within life, and always from the point of view of some specific becoming.

Deleuze insists that we move beyond a limited point of view of good and evil (or from a point of view that *judges life*) to an expanded point of view that sees all values as effects of the flow of life. This means moving beyond morality – where we assume that the world has a system of good and evil oppositions – to ethics, where we create and select those powers that expand life as a whole, beyond our limited perspectives. We create and select not on the basis of who we *are* (for this would install a value or end within life) but how we might become (extending life to its fullest potential). Our becoming is enhanced if we free ourselves from the illusion of transcendence – the illusion that there is a ground or law other than ourselves (or within ourselves) that simply needs to be obeyed or revealed. A maximised becoming is a commitment to univocity, affirming all those differences and creations which traverse us, including the genetic, historical and affect-ive investments that have constituted us but do not define us once and for all.

Most importantly, univocity, immanence and transcendentalism preclude us from making a dualist opposition between the actual and the virtual. Western thought has tended to ignore the virtual power of becoming (which is potentiality or what is not-yet). It does this by arguing that we begin with an actual world, which already contains all future possibilities, and possibility would just be what we imagine might have happened. Possibility would be less than the actual and not a power in its own right. Evolution, on this picture, would be a mere unfolding of already given possibilities, a progression towards an already determined end. For Deleuze, however, univocity means insisting on the actual and the virtual as fully real, with the virtual being at least an equal power. Life for Deleuze is a virtual power, the power to become: not towards some already given end or on the basis of what already (actually) is. Virtual difference has the power to become in unforeseen ways, always *more* that this actual world, and not limited by its already present forms. Virtual potentiality is more than this actual world, unlike possibility which we think of as less than fully real or as what might have taken place but did not (Deleuze 1988c). From virtual tendencies or potentialities certain beings are actualised. Genes, for example, actualise themselves in distinct bodies but also harness powers for further mutation and becoming beyond the body which expresses them; such becomings may or may not be actualised but they are nevertheless fully real and part of the one flow of life. Whereas possibility is a pale and imagined version of the actual world, virtual difference and becoming is the very power of the world. Any actual being is traversed by the virtual, not just what it might become but also its variation in relation to other becomings. An organism is a variation of the life that passes through it, but it also varies in response to other organisms. If we step back from our perception of distinct and closed actual organisms we can intuit the one virtual life of difference and variation of which they are expressions.

SIMULACRA

Today, when we use the words 'virtual reality', we speak as though there is an actual or real world that simply *is* and then its virtual or unreal copy. We also often think of the world today as 'postmodern' because it has lost all relation with the actual world and is dominated by copies and images. The postmodern world is caught up in television, advertising, copies of designer goods, cloning, the meaningless repetition of brand-names and computer simulations of just about everything. Whether we celebrate or lament this world, we nevertheless describe it through a distinction between the actual and the virtual: there was once a time when we were close to reality (which is actual) and now all we have are images (the virtual). This is why, following contemporary thinkers like Jean Baudrillard, postmodern culture has been described as a society of 'simulacra'.

One of the most often-cited literary instances of the simulacrum is the 'most photographed barn in America' in Don Delillo's great postmodern novel, *White Noise* (1985). The barn has become a tourist attraction because it has been photographed so many times; so what is being photographed, or what the tourists are going to see, is not what the barn *is* in its concrete reality, but what the barn has become through repeated simulation. The barn is a simulacra precisely because it has no origin. You can only photograph the most photographed barn in America *after* it has been photographed; the process of imaging and simulation precedes and produces what the barn is. It becomes photographable (as the 'most photographed') only through the process of photography. From a Baudrillardian point of view this is lamentable. We have lost all relation with actual barns − their place in farm life

JEAN BAUDRILLARD (1929–)

A French cultural theorist whose dominant concern has been the post-modern turn to simulation or 'hyperreality'. For Baudrillard the dominance of simulacra in postmodern culture is symptomatic of a loss of the real. We no longer have the ability to distinguish between the real world and its images. Advertising, for example, today sells us images rather than things; we buy the label or sign of Chanel, Calvin Klein or GAP rather than any quality or value this label represents. Baudrillard's most notorious pronouncement was that the Gulf War 'did not take place'. What he meant by this was that the media had so anticipated and dominated the event that the war had no *place* or real location, precisely because the war was won through images. Not only was there a war of images, where presen-tations of the Middle East were deployed to demonise the enemy, missiles were sent and tracked using imaging devices, the CNN television viewer could see the war as a media event while it was occurring. The place of the war was no longer limited, but extended to every Western television screen – to the point where a distinction could not be made between the sending of weapons and the sending of images. In such a world, Baudrillard argues, we have lost the power of critique. We cannot measure the virtual image against the actual world, because we have lost all sense of the actual.

and rural culture – and fallen into a world where we value something only to the extent to which it has been copied. Against this rigid distinc-tion between the actual and the virtual Deleuze argues that the real is always actual–virtual. First, any 'actual' being is already an image. The supposed first barn, for example, would already have been built from some idea or image of a barn. An actual thing is produced only from virtual possibilities. There must already be some general image of a barn in order to build, recognise and perceive an actual barn. Second, our 'real' world is actual–virtual. It is not just that the actual world is the effect of virtual potential, each actual thing maintains its own virtual power. What something is (actually) is also its power to become (virtually). The barn, for example, can become a tourist attraction, a photograph and any number of other possibilities. We tend to think that we have an actual world which precedes simulation, but for Deleuze there is an 'original' process of simulation. Beings or things emerge from processes of copying, doubling, imaging and simulation.

Each unique work of art or each human individual is a simulation: genes copy and repeat, with deviation, while art works become singular not by *being* the world but by transforming it through images that are at once actual and virtual.

We only realise virtual potentialities after they have been actualised. We never see the virtual or the power of simulation itself; we see created beings but not the process of becoming of which they are actual affects. We see creativity from already given works of art, but this does not stop us imagining creations of the future. We study genetics from already constituted organisms, but this does not stop us from seeing the potential for not-actual genetic mutations and creations. We only have actual beings – from artworks to organisms – because of the virtual power of becoming. And an actual being is also a virtual dimension; a plant is not just its matter but is also a need or expectation of light and water. So, instead of dividing the world between an actual reality and its unreal virtual copy Deleuze argues for a world of simulacra. There is not an original life that is then varied or copied in different versions; each event of life is already other than itself, not original, a simulation.

An ethics committed to univocity is therefore an ethics of potentialities. We increase our power, not by affirming our *actual* being – 'I am human, recognise me' – but by expanding our perception to those virtual powers that we are not – the creation of a 'people to come'. Literature is a power of affirmation and potentiality only if it is viewed not as the *representation* of the world, but as the expression and creation of what is not yet, not present or other than the actual. Literature gives us other worlds and becomings. It does so, not by being a copy of the actual world, but by extending the virtual tendencies of the given world. We should not represent an image of what thinking is, but maximise the power of producing new and previously unimagined styles of thinking. Literature is simulation or the power of the simulacra, the power to produce appearances, images and styles that are not grounded on anything other than their own becoming. In *Difference and Repetition* (1994) Deleuze cites Fyodor Dostoevsky's (1821–81) 'Underground man' from *Notes from Underground* (1864). The work is written as a diary, even though the underground man continually insists that he does not want to be read or understood. The whole style of the work is a paradox: a voice that insists, over and over, on not being heard. Further, the underground man presents a series of scenes in which he flouts convention, manners and all the bourgeois rituals of conformity *at the same time* that he insists on being included within the social circles he acknowledges to be worthless. The underground man perverts the very logic of speech. To speak is, necessarily, to submit to a shared language, culture and at least some degree of sociability. The underground man corrupts this logic; he lies, contradicts himself, yells that he does not want to be heard and argues against the coherence of arguments. Instead of presenting us with the image of human reason the Underground man exaggerates the powers of disagreement, misrecognition, inconsistency and a transcendental or excessive malevolence and stupidity. The stupidity is transcendental because it destroys the idea of an organising reason. Instead we see the power of thought to create ridiculous, ungrounded and bizarre connections with no end or purpose.

Against the idea that there is an actual world and its virtual copy, we have said, Deleuze argues for the simulacrum. What any thing *is* is its power to become other, to produce fake or masked images of itself, to *not* be faithful to itself. The idea of 'copy' presupposes some original model and Western thought has been dominated by the figure of the copy: the idea that there are originals that can be used to measure and judge claimants (Deleuze 1994). We ask if this is *really* 'justice', 'democracy' or 'literature' – imagining that there is some model or standard of which these instances are copies or repetitions. We often speak of a person's 'character' as some peculiarity, style or variation that is added on to some otherwise basic human sameness. But to insist, as Deleuze does, that life is *just* simulation is to insist that we are nothing other than the characters or masks that we play. It is to insist that there is no 'model' of justice or literature outside each invention and creation of just or literary events. It is not that we have a self that we *then* conceal or express through simulation or performance, nor is it the case that there is an essence of literature that can be used to judge future literary creations. The idea of an original or underlying self or essence is the *effect* of the produced masks and copies. The simulacrum produces the effect of an original, producing new selves and originals with each performance.

We often seem to lament the fact that today we live in a world of simulations: that events such as the Gulf War, presidential elections or 'real life' television begin as media events and have no real substance. Postmodern literature is often defined as a movement that merely quotes or parodies styles and images without ever saying or referring to anything. As noted above, Jean Baudrillard argues that media culture has reduced everything to surface images with no reference to the real. Deleuze's notion of the simulacra both resists the nostalgia that would want to go back to a time when life was 'more real' *and* rejects the idea that we now live in a postmodern world of mere images with no real causes. For Deleuze the simulacrum or image is real, and life is and always has been simulation – a power of production, creation becoming and difference. The idea that all we have are mere representations or constructions of the world seems to posit some real world that is lost or unavailable. Whether we mourn or celebrate the postmodern loss of the real, both models assume that the simulacrum is not real, a mere copy. The simulacrum for Deleuze, however, is neither a recent nor a merely cultural event. The simulacrum is not the loss or abandonment of the real; it *is* the real. A force of life becomes by enhancing its powers of variation and its powers of being affected; it takes on a form other than what it is. It imagines or projects what it is not (yet). It simulates: becoming other than itself through the very power of a life which is always more than itself. If literature is a power of the simulacrum it is not because it merely quotes or parodies with no respect for the real; it is because it produces new simulations, a new expression of the real.

SUMMARY

Ideology explains the way in which individuals abandon their desires for the sake of some illusory higher end. Ideology gives a negative and repressive account of power. Against the idea that desire is repressed by some separate power that is other than desire, Deleuze argues that desire produces terms which it can then (mistakenly) posit as powers to be obeyed. Affirming desire does not mean doing away with power, but does require that we see any supposedly separate law or point of judgement as part of one immanent plane of desire. Revolution begins, not with the removal of power to reveal what lies behind power, but by seeing power as productive, creative and with no ordering or external end: this means seeing power as desire not as law. Logically, there can only be one being. Being must be univocal. Any attempt to think a world divided into higher and lesser beings would have to posit a point of order or reason outside being, a point of judgement. But any such point is itself part of being and life. From the affirmation of one single being thought expands to an ethics of pluralism, where each becoming is an expression of life. Ethically, the task for both philosophy and art is the creation and maximisation of becoming against the *recognition* of becoming in any of its actualised terms. This is an ethics of the simulacra: the affirmation of variation without ground, of the repetition of difference with no end or reason outside itself.

6

MINOR LITERATURE

The power of eternal return

In this chapter we will be looking at Deleuze's more specific comments on literature, and how literature opens out into the political issues of sense, the virtual, simulation and cultural imagination. In particular, we will see why, for Deleuze, we need to approach literature as *minor* literature. We have already seen that Deleuze distinguishes art from philosophy and science. Art has the power, not to represent the world or located subjects, but to imagine, create and vary affects that are not already given. In literature, for example, such affects would be the powers of language that are not tied down to communication and representation, a language that becomes sound (a stuttering language) or a language that creates sense (such as the absurd world of *Alice in Wonderland*). Such a literature, Deleuze and Guattari argue, is a *minor* literature. It does not appeal to established models; nor does it claim to represent humanity. It produces what is not already recognisable. It does not just add one more work to the great tradition; it disrupts and dislocates the tradition. Deleuze and Guattari describe the project of minor literature in their book on Franz Kafka (1883–1924), published in French in 1975, precisely because Kafka was a Czech Jew who wrote in German (Deleuze and Guattari 1986). He did not occupy a language or culture that he could consider his own or identical with his being. All great literature, for Deleuze and Guattari, is minor in this sense: language seems foreign, open to mutation, and the vehicle for the *creation* of identity rather than the *expression* of identity.

MAJORITARIAN/MINORITARIAN

Throughout their major work, *A Thousand Plateaus*, Deleuze and Guattari draw a distinction between minoritarian and majoritarian. Like all their 'distinctions' what looks like a simple opposition is far more complex. Minoritarian and majoritarian are ways of drawing distinctions. A majoritarian mode, for example, presents the opposition as already given and based on a privileged and original term. So, 'man' is a majoritarian term; we imagine that there is some general being – the human – that then has local variations: such as racial, sexual or cultural variations. The opposition between man and woman is majoritarian: we think of woman as other than, or different from, man. A minoritarian mode of difference does not ground the distinction on a privileged term, and does not see the distinction as an already-given order. Deleuze and Guattari describe 'woman' or 'becoming-woman' as minoritarian (Deleuze and Guattari 1987). This is not because women are a minority; it is because, for the most part, there is no standard or norm for woman. If we really acknowledge the possibility that there is something like becoming-woman, then we acknowledge that there is something truly other than man: that human life is not defined by the male ideals of reason, strength, dominance and activity. 'Woman' opens the human to new possibilities. 'Woman' is a minoritarian term only if it remains an open term in becoming, as it was in the early days of the women's movement when there was much contestation about just what women were fighting for. Once a term becomes expressive, rather than creative, of identity it becomes majoritarian. Once 'woman' is appealed to as a new standard, as the embodiment of caring, nurturing, passivity or compassion it becomes majoritarian: capable of excluding those who do not fulfil the criteria.

Literature, when it fully extends its power of being literature, is always minoritarian. Minor literature is great literature, not necessarily the literature of minorities, although this can be the case. Kafka was a great writer, not because he captured the unrepresented spirit of the Czech people, but because he wrote without a standard notion of 'the people'. He wrote, not as a being with an identity, but as a voice of what is not given, a 'people to come'. But the same goes for all great writing. Shakespeare can be considered a 'minor' author precisely because his works do not offer a unified image of man, or even a unified image of Shakespeare. His texts are more like question marks, with each production or reading raising new questions. Of course, when Shakespeare becomes an industry (of tourism, culture and academia) he becomes a major author: we seek to find the real Shakespeare, the origin of his ideas and the true sense of his works. He becomes minor, again, only if we recognise the potential in his work to be read as if we did not know who Shakespeare was.

THE IDEA OF LITERATURE

From the very beginning Deleuze affirmed the power of the *Idea* of literature (where an Idea is not what is actually given; it is not a generalisation, but rather what we can think beyond any actual or already given experience). Typically, for Deleuze, there is no unified theory of the literary. He does not argue, for example, that literature is the expression of an author's intent; nor is it the reflection or distortion of the world; nor can literature be reduced to the sense made of it by its readers. In *What is Philosophy?* Deleuze and Guattari want to mark the *difference* of literature: not what literature *is* so much as the forces or powers of becoming that it reveals. Unlike science, which takes the flow of life and fixes it into observable 'states of affairs' that can be ordered by functions, and unlike philosophy which creates concepts in order to think the immanence of becoming, literature moves in its own direction or *tendency*. We may always see in any literary text mixtures of the scientific or philosophical tendencies. Just as humans are composites of animality and imagination, and animals are composites of matter and consciousness, so a literary text also contains scientific powers of observation and reference and philosophical powers of conceptuality. But while the human is never pure consciousness, the human nevertheless *extends* the tendency of consciousness, realising it beyond any of its animal expressions. It is in human life that consciousness forms an image of itself, reflects upon itself and thereby maximises the very power of consciousness. Similarly, it is in literature that the component of affect comes into its own right. All discourses may have an affective component. A scientist might produce a moving or even tear-provoking image of the origin of life, but what makes science scientific is not its power to affect but its power to functionalise life. And this is a tendency, not a general or common feature. Each scientific function and each philosophical concept realises its tendencies in its own way.

Deleuze identifies the tendency of art to be the production of affects and percepts. This might seem to privilege the visual arts. It is much easier to imagine a painter or film-maker presenting colour and texture in their singularity, freed of all meaning, order or reference, than it is to imagine a work of literature as affect. Insofar as literature uses language it is hard to see how it could avoid signification or representation. Certainly, Deleuze refers throughout his work to the visual arts and wrote a book on sensation exploring the work of the twentieth-century artist Francis Bacon (Deleuze 1981). But we need to be careful not to reduce the *virtual* notion of affect to the immediate experience of sensible data. Affect occurs not just when the eye is confronted by colour, but when this seeing gives us the thought or image of that virtual difference that allows colour to be given, not just *as given to us* in this *affection*, but as anonymous *affect*. We 'see' the colours of the art-work, not just within our world, but as there to be seen, as visual, as powers of the sensible. Literature for Deleuze has its own singular power of affect, one quite different from the visual arts. What is realised in literary affect is not this or that message, not this or that speaker, but the power that allows for speaking and saying – freed from any subject of enunciation.

Deleuze therefore offers a unique approach to style. It is not that there is a world of speakers with meanings and messages that they convey *through style*. Rather, there are styles or creations that allow for speech, and it is from each event of speech that a speaking position or speaker is actualised. Style is best thought of as virtual, as a power of variation and becoming, a power to create anew without prior reference or ground. Deleuze offered a number of ways to think about the literary approach to intensities and affect. Each event of the literary re-opens the question of what and how literature might become, and so each mobilisation and creation of affect is itself different. Style is not the external or accidental adornment of a message; it is the creation of affects *from which* speakers and messages are discerned.

SIGNS AND INTENSITIES

We have already seen how some forms of literature can have a diagnostic power in their description of *affects*. Characters are not harmonious and unified substances but assemblages or 'refrains': a collection of body-parts, gestures, desires and motifs. Each character therefore opens out on to a unique world or becoming, a unique way of moving through life and connecting with life. The character we encounter is a sign, but not of something that we might know or experience so much as a sign of an entirely different 'line' of experience or becoming. In addition to the presentation of affects, literature can also explore language itself as affect. This is where language is not meaning or message but closer to the dimension of noise, music or sonorous style. This helps us to understand how, for Deleuze, affect is at once singular and collective. Affect is singular because it has no reason or justification, no order or relation, outside itself. The Western investment in whiteness is singular – the investment in a specific intensity that is then made meaningful and justified after the event; it becomes a sign of reason and civilisation. Whiteness becomes the signifier for rationality and humanity; but the whole point of Deleuze's method is to say that these supposedly *signified* qualities that affects represent are the effects, not the grounds. It is not the case that there is the dominance of 'the West' which then leads to the elevation of white skin; it is the investments in the affects of white skin, in a style of thought, in certain bodies and gestures and so on that produces the West. We begin with an investment, say, in the white, phallic, powerful, active body and *then* elevate it as a 'signifier' of law or 'man' in general.

Throughout his works Deleuze was critical of the concept of language as a 'signifier', as proposed by the structuralists, for this suggests that there is a world (referent), the meanings we impose or find in that world (signifieds) and then the tokens or sounds we use to systematise those meanings (signifiers). The notion of language as signification is one of transcendence: we assume an outside world that is then re-presented through a separate system of signs. We think of language as the representation, construction or organisation of some 'outside' world, so language starts to act as a privileged and independent subject or agent. Deleuze made two broad responses to this.

First, there is not a present world and then a representing language. The world or cosmos is an immanent plane of signification or 'semiosis'; there are signs and codes throughout life, not just in the separate mind of man or language. Genetic codes; an insect 'reading' a plant; the stomach decomposing and 'analysing' nutrients; and a computer chewing through information and data: all these inhuman variations and selections are chains of code and response. It is the myth of representation that separates man from an inert and passive world that he then brings to language. Second, before signs are representative and extensive, they are *intensive*. Before there is a system of language that allows us to refer to a world stretched out before us, there are investments in intensities. A tribe, for example, enjoys and invests in an image, such as an animal, a body-part or an inscription. It is not that the tribe uses the symbol of the animal to represent who they are; it is only in gathering around or desiring this image that there is a tribe at all. The investment *produces* an assemblage of bodies; it does not represent it. Deleuze and Guattari refer to these as 'territorial' or collective investments, and it is the investment that connects the tribe as a group – not some underlying identity, which the investment then signifies. By looking and enjoying, each eye of the tribe invests in an image. From this intensive investment, where images and inscriptions are *enjoyed*, these images become signifiers by being 'overcoded'. This can happen when the enjoyed image becomes a sign *of* some social meaning: the body looked upon by the tribe becomes a punished or venerated body. There is no longer a single level of freely floating images; images are seen or read as the signs *of* some meaning and are referred to some subject who 'reads' that meaning. Eventually this process of 'overcoding' produces social machines and 'man'. Investments or affective enjoyments are read as signs and we take these signs to be representative *of* some pre-existing real; we then assume that there is a humanity which precedes the encounter of investments and assemblages. For example, when tribes come into relation with each other their specific investments can be read as signs of some underlying human culture – we are all tribes as instances *of* the human. But referral of intensities *back* to some underlying reality would require some 'overcoding' point of view of the anthropologist who would *interpret* each specific tribe as a signifier of man in general.

In modern cultures we think of all signs as 'signifiers', as signs *of* some underlying sense or as referable back to some speaking subject. (If there is a sign there must be someone who means something and some object that is signified.) We no longer think of language as intensive and effective, as in the chants, rhythms and incantations of primitive cultures. We think of signs as signifiers, and we think of language as communication or information (representation). We think of language as a vehicle for messages among speakers, rather than as a creative and intensive event that produces speakers. Deleuze, by contrast, wants to show how speakers are the *effect* of investments in language. This can be shown in free-indirect style and the infinitive.

INDIRECT DISCOURSE AND THE INFINITIVE

One of the common appeals that Deleuze makes to literature is its power of indirect and especially free-indirect discourse. Indirect discourse reports a saying or speaking that 'comes from outside': 'it is said that . . .'; 'it was thought that. . . .' Free-indirect discourse is more complex. It uses third person narration but speaks in the received, common or clichéd style of the characters described, so it is neither the author or the character who is speaking. We describe the character in the style that they might use. Franz Kafka's story, 'Metamorphosis', of 1916, about Gregor Samsa who wakes up to find himself transformed into an insect, concludes with the picture of Gregor's family after Gregor's pathetic death. It is written in the very style of the bourgeois family and 'happy endings'. It is neither Kafka nor some specific character who is narrating the following paragraph; it is spoken in the style of trite conclusions and a life that will always go an as normal:

> The greatest immediate improvement in their condition would of course arise from moving to another house; they would have to take a smaller and cheaper but also better situated and more easily run apartment than the one they had, which Gregor had selected. While they were thus conversing, it struck both Mr. and Mrs. Samsa, almost at the same moment, as they became aware of their daugher's increasing vivacity, that in spite of all the sorrow of recent times, which had made her cheeks pale, she had bloomed into a pretty girl with a good figure. They grew quieter and half unconsciously exchanged glances of complete agreement, having come to the conclusion that it would soon be time to find a good husband for her. And it was like a confirmation of their new dreams and excellent intentions that at the end of their journey their daughter sprung to her feet and stretched her young body.
>
> (Kafka 1961: 62–3)

Note the use of 'smaller and cheaper but also better situated', 'excellent intentions' and 'a pretty girl with a good figure': all these are phrases of a voice of unquestioning middle-class ordinariness. It is as though the girl's young body is already stifled by the dead language of bourgeois morality. There is a clear absurdity in this narration of 'normality' after the previous descriptions of a family living with a man–insect, as though moving house and finding good husbands were 'excellent intentions' or appropriate responses to a situation as bizarre as theirs had been. Free-indirect style presents characters through the styles of language they might use. In such cases the boundary between author and character is undecidable; we are never certain who is speaking, the author or the author in the style of the character. The infinitive, like indirect and free-indirect discourse, also complicates the relation between speakers and language. While indirect discourse shows that ways of speaking do not originate in characters – for we all receive language from elsewhere – the infinitive speaks without a subject altogether. Instead of 'I dance' or 'he dances', there is just the pure potential of 'to dance', not restricted by any agent of subject *who dances*. (In French infinitives are often single words. 'To think' is '*penser*', so the English equivalent might just be the impersonal 'thinking'.)

Western thought, and the logic of transcendence, presupposes the model of language as a proposition or judgement. There is a subject who observes the world and then predicates certain qualities of that world in statements. The proposition form, S is P, posits a subject or substance as a being, which then has certain qualities: 'the tree is green'. The infinitive, however, like the verb, places the potential for action and event before the being it actualises. Instead of 'the tree is green', it would be better to think of distinct becomings or potentialities, such as 'to green', or 'to tree'. For Deleuze, this mobilisation of language away from propositions is the event of sense. Sense is virtual and incorporeal, and is a power of bodies that goes beyond what bodies *actually* are. For example, Captain' Cook's *Endeavour* landed in Australia in 1770, but when this meeting of land and ship was called a 'discovery' or 'landing' or 'settlement' an event of sense occurred. It had the power to transform bodies, both of those who landed and of those who were displaced. When indigenous Australians later referred to the 1770 event as an 'invasion' they also created an event of sense, and also transformed what bodies could do. Indigenous peoples were able to occupy land when 'Australia' was no longer regarded as a blank space to be overtaken ('terra nullius'), and the

Aboriginal peoples themselves were also no longer regarded as bodies to be managed so much as voices with a vote, rights and histories. Language is not about representation, naming or propositions, but rather about creating worlds of sense that interact with other material worlds, such as those of bodies, laws and cultures. Infinitives, free-indirect style and new names bring us closer to the power of language to allow events and movements. Transforming Australian politics would not just mean giving the land an Aboriginal name, for the production of Australia as a common whole occurs with its creation as some single thing *to be named*. Infinitives allow language to be seen, not as naming but as doing. For Aboriginal peoples, land is not so much an object to be named as it is the possibility or potential for action: a place for walking, dreaming, painting and assembling.

Language can operate actively or reactively to the incorporeal trans-formations of sense. Reactively, it can present itself as mere descrip-tion, as a simple recognition or proposition about a world that remains the same, and that language merely doubles. Actively, it can extend and express its transformative power, and for Deleuze language does this most in literature. Deleuze cites, in particular, the *nonsense* literature of Lewis Carroll. Carroll freed events and becomings from their actual and material bearers, such as the 'smile without a cat' in *Alice's Adventures in Wonderland*. Through the use of nonsense Carroll also displayed the emergence of sense. Words like 'snark' in *The Hunting of the Snark* are not labels or descriptions that we attach to the world; they have no already given meaning. Carroll's literature creates imaginary animals, and disembodied events by combining language in new ways. It affirms language as active creation, rather than reactive representation.

Sense, for Deleuze, is the virtual milieu through which we live and become. Sense is not reducible to the 'meanings' of a language; sense is what allows a language to be meaningful. For example, words like 'gay', 'queer', 'straight' or 'bi' and so on only have meaning because of the modern sense of sexuality. It would be impossible to translate the word 'gay' into Ancient Greek or old English, not because they lacked an equivalent word, but because they did not approach the world through the *problem* or sense of 'sexuality' (the problem of 'my' inner sexual self above and beyond my bodily acts). Sense is not just the collection of words of a language, nor is it the bodies named; it is the way we think or approach those bodies. It is because we think of each body as having its own personal sexuality that the statements of sexual psychology *make sense*. Speaking and thinking, or what we take the world to be, rest less on judgements and propositions than the action of a question. Deleuze says that this is not being or non-being but '?being' (Deleuze 1994). In poetry and nonsense literature we do not just see language as description; we see *language's power to transform itself through sense*. When Carroll, for example, combines two part words into a 'portmanteau' word, he does not simply add two meanings; a new sense is produced.

FREE INDIRECT STYLE

Again, in contrast to the proposition which assumes a subject who represents a world, indirect speech begins collectively or 'tribally'. Think of the way, for the most part, everyday language 'comes from elsewhere' or is indirect. Even a simple exchange – 'Hello' – 'How are you?' – 'Fine, and you?' – is not something authored by the speaker. Most language takes this indirect form of an 'it is said that . . .'; and the 'I' who speaks is, Deleuze argues, an *effect* of a certain way of speaking. It is in free-indirect style that literature discloses language as a 'collective assemblage'. It is not that there are speakers who then adopt specific styles; styles produce speaking positions.

Consider the following sentence that opens James Joyce's 'A Painful Case' from *Dubliners*:

> Mr James Duffy lived in Chapelizod because he wished to live as far as possible from the city of which he was a citizen and because he found all the other suburbs of Dublin mean, modern and pretentious.
>
> (James Joyce 1977: 89)

Although the sentence is written in third person narration it uses the language of the character it describes. To refer to suburbs as 'mean, modern and pretentious' is to speak from a position of conservative, dismissive and judgemental moralism, where 'modern' becomes a pejorative. As so often in *Dubliners*, although the sentence is not actually quoted, the way of speaking is already typical of a place, rather than a subject. To use the words 'mean, modern and pretentious' or to speak of 'citizens' is to show the ways in which Dublin is already a certain lexicon. The sentence is written in the 'voice' of Dublin. This is why all minor literature is directly political: not because it expresses a political message but because its mode of articulation takes voice away from the speaking subject to an anonymous or pre-personal saying. Joyce's style, for example, is less the expression of an individual subject than it is the articulation of what Deleuze and Guattari refer to as a 'collective assemblage'. Instead of establishing a transcendent position outside life – a higher moralism – free-indirect style repeats the language of Dublin from within, showing its own limits. Characters like Mr Duffy are produced and enslaved by their way of speaking, which is also a way of perceiving. The tone of judgement and moralism separated Mr Duffy from a world, which he looks down upon. As its title suggests, Joyce's *Dubliners* is about a territory, about Dublin as a series of ways of speaking. The narration is not in quotation marks, so we do not get the sense of this speech being owned by any particular subject. Often what is *said* throughout *Dubliners* is not intended, but seems to pass through characters in an almost mechanical or inhuman way. One character refers to 'rheumatic wheels', while another story ('The Dead') begins with the sentence, 'Lily, the caretaker's daughter, was literally run off her feet (James Joyce 1977: 138). Wheels can't be rheumatic and you cannot *literally* be run off your feet.

Free-indirect style repeats the nonsense or noise of everyday language, showing how language circulates as affect. It is not that we speak in a certain way *because* of our beliefs or ideas. Rather, there are styles of speaking, phrases and rhythms that produce us beyond any *conscious* or intended decisions; it is the style of life and becoming, and not meanings or messages, that creates us as desiring subjects. One story in *Dubliners*, 'Grace', describes a group of businessmen who use a religious terminology to refer to their 'calling', while their parish priest refers to religion in terms of 'settling accounts'. The narrative voice of Joyce's story sees its characters' commercial exploits through the language of the Christian faith: as a dignified 'calling' with 'offices' a 'crusade' and even baptismal metaphors of 'brief immersions in the waters of general philosophy' (Joyce 1977: 122–7). The Christian 'message' that concludes the story is expressed in the vocabulary of accountancy: 'Well, I have verified my accounts. I find all well'. The characters, here, are produced through the language of business and religion, languages that are shown to be essentially capable of contamination, confusion and mutation. Free-indirect style shows how language frees itself from speakers and intentions. Dublin, for Joyce, was not a national spirit or Irish character that simply needed to be expressed through language. A people is an event of language, a 'collective assemblage'. Language has its own affective power, above and beyond meaning. Religion, in nearly all Joyce's writing, circulates in the way that football chants, popular songs and advertising slogans are repeated – as noise and intensity rather than 'signification'. When we sing a team song or utter a phrase such as 'Everything happens for a reason', we are usually *not* saying or meaning anything at all. We are repeating the slogans or refrains that compose us.

Literature therefore opens out in two directions from free-indirect style. First, it diagnoses the affects and intensities that create us. In the case of Joyce, he shows how Dublin as a territory is composed of a religious moralism and a bourgeois commercialism. Second, there is also the positive dimension of sense. Once free-indirect style frees language from its ownership by any subject of enunciation, we can see the flow of language itself, its production of sense and nonsense, its virtual and creative power. This is why free-indirect style merges with stream of consciousness. Free-indirect style uses the third person to describe single characters from the point of view of a received and anonymous language. It shows that who we are is an effect of our style of speech, and that our styles and habits are always perceived from elsewhere. (Life pulses through us; it is not something we own.) It is not the 'I' that lies at the origin of language but an anonymous 'it is said that. . . .' Stream of consciousness takes this a step further, taking language away from even a collective assemblage, such as the territory of modern Dublin. Language becomes a flow, list, voice or series of affects that do not so much 'say' or 'mean' as *produce* a passage from noise to word, from sound to sense.

BLOCKS OF BECOMING

While free-indirect style diagnoses the specific territories of language, literature can also move towards 'absolute deterritorialisation' where sensations and affects are freed from subjects of speech and judgement. Deleuze and Guattari refer to Virginia Woolf in this regard, especially her novel *The Waves*. Unlike Joyce in *Dubliners* (but like the Joyce of *Ulysses*) Woolf is no longer diagnosing a limited way of speaking that produces a certain style of person. She creates styles of direct affect. If art is the creation of affect, or the experience of sensibility independent of its actual organisation, how can *language* be art? Surely language is always meaningful or conceptual? The *art* of language would need to disclose the possibility or virtual potential of language, its power to create and encounter, rather than its already constituted forms. Deleuze addresses this problem of the literary throughout his work, with Woolf forming a privileged case in *A Thousand Plateaus*.

It is banal everyday opinion that passes directly from what we see or perceive to what we say, from the visible world to the production of sense. Opinion speaks as though the sensible experience of life were already meaningful, present and beyond question, requiring only the recognition of language. Opinion takes the form of, 'I don't like this; therefore this is bad'. It moves directly from the sensible to sense, assuming a shared 'we' who would all agree in this judgement (Deleuze and Guattari 1994). The *art* of literature disengages sense from the sensible. In Woolf's *The Waves* perception struggles towards sense. Language 'stutters', to use Deleuze's phrase. Stream of consciousness presents words, perceptions, received noises, quotations and connectives, without any external organising subject of narration. In Woolf this takes two directions. Often there is a dislocation of affect from any character, but there is also a dislocation of percept from any object. In *The Waves* descriptions of sensible percepts (what is received or intuited) intertwine with characters' affects (what is felt). Frequently it is difficult or impossible to determine *who* is feeling what, or what is being sensed. Flows of colours, images, sensations cross the text, with sentences being neither clearly attributable to an external narrator, nor to a described character. Deleuze and Guattari describe this as 'blocks of becoming' (Deleuze and Guattari 1987: 277). There is not a being who then becomes, but tendencies to become which produce differences that are not differences *between* distinct beings: 'Movements, becomings, in other words, pure relations of speed and slowness, pure affects, are below and above the threshold of perception' (Deleuze and Guattari 1987: 281). There is no harmonious ordering of a world perceived, a subject affected and a language that signifies this experience. On the contrary, 'percepts' and 'affects' are listed, rather than ordered from a separate point of view. Literature becomes affect, an impersonal rhythm, sound or tone – *moving towards* designating a world.

MINOR LITERATURE

Literature is important, for Deleuze and Guattari, not because of the messages it sends us, but because it has the power to take us away from the coded messages of language back to the sounds, marks and affects from which meanings emerge. Deleuze and Guattari argue that there are systems of inscription (marking or writing) well before meaning or signification. They insist on a pre-history of sense, on the emergence of human language and meaning from primitive and bodily relations. A tribe is formed through inscription, tattooing, incision or body painting. There is not yet an underlying identity which these marks are assumed to represent; the assemblage is nothing outside these marks, and these marks or scars are not the signs *of* anything other than themselves. After this event of assemblage or territorialisation, these marks can be 'read' as signs *of* some general identity. This occurs when one body sets itself outside the tribe and presents itself as representative of a social order, which the marks are now taken to represent. A despot emerges from the tribe and posits himself as a figure of law and origin descended from the gods. The marks then become signs *of* a belonging that has some external reference point (the body of the despot). The territory is *de*territorialised. It is now more than an assemblage of bodies. One body has 'leapt outside the chain' and presented itself as origin, meaning or law of the assemblage. Something like this also explains the function of language as signification. Language begins as a system of marks or affective inscriptions, non-signifying signs (the sounds, letters and material differences). But these marks can be freed from their origin and become deterritorialised to produce sense; we can read the mark as the sign of some meaning which is not the mark itself. A word has the power to articulate a sense regardless of who speaks; sense can only occur when the word is not just a sound *I* make, but is taken as a *word*, a sense that 'we' would all recognise. So language occurs with the deterritorialisation of marks; marks no longer refer directly to the body that utters or bears them; marks are signs of a sense we all share, above and beyond any single inscription. Language is essentially deterritorialised, collective, tribal or detached from any single body or speaker. By freeing signs from any single origin, deterritorialisation allows us to speak; we can communicate and become speakers in a collective assemblage. *Re*territorialisation occurs when we imagine a subject who was there all along at the origin of language. We think that 'man' invented language, rather than being one of language's effects.

We have seen how free-indirect style deterritorialises language by showing its emergence as noise or affect above and beyond any speaker's intention. But there is another way of approaching language as 'collective assemblage', and that is through Deleuze and Guattari's notion of a minor literature. They make a distinction between subject groups and subjugated groups, and this is directly connected to the politics of style. In keeping with transcendental empiricism we need to think of language as an act or event that produces the effect of underlying speakers or subjects. There are no speakers or subjects who precede the event of their becoming. A subject group forms as an act of speech or a demand, as an event of becoming. (Imagine, for example, the inauguration of the women's movement, which began by speaking differently, by *not* recognising the norms of male reason.) The subject group forms itself *through* speaking or becoming. (The women's movement was, from its very beginning, a literary movement, the very notion of 'woman' being created through novels and women's writing.) A *subjugated* group, by contrast, speaks as though it were representing, rather than forming, its identity. This occurs when, say, we start to think of women's writing as the expression of an underlying femininity that was lying in wait for literary inscription. The group becomes subjugated to an image of its own identity; its becoming is no longer open but is seen as the becoming *of* some specific essence. Writing becomes prescriptive and *majoritarian*; it is now based upon an identity and demands *recognition*, rather than the constitution, of that identity.

The distinction between minorities and majorities (or between a molecular and molar politics) is therefore not one of numbers, but of *types* of quantity. A majoritarian identity has established its extended unit of measure – its notion of a proper or representative number. It makes no difference how many men or humans there are; we all still know what 'man' is. This is an extensive multiplicity. Adding more members does not alter what the group or multiplicity is. It is therefore possible for humanity to include or recognise women or blacks as 'equal'. It did so, not by changing its notion of the human (as rational, individual and goal-oriented), but by arguing that women and blacks could also be rational, democratic, economically-motivated and moral, 'just like us'.

A minoritarian politics does not have a pre-given (or transcendent) measure or norm for inclusion or identity. Each addition to the group changed what the group is. (When non-middle-class women were included in the women's movement feminism had to change its image of femininity as domestic, well-mannered, refined and 'lady-like' to include women who worked and laboured outside the home. When women of colour were included this led to a challenging of women being 'equal' to men, for many of the norms of masculinity were tied to white Western culture.) An intensive multiplicity cannot increase or decrease without changing its quality. You add more light to a colour and it becomes a different colour. This is an intensive multiplicity. You take one red thing out of a box of red things and you still have a box of red things. This is an extensive multiplicity. Following on from this, a minor literature does not write to express what it *is* (as though it had an identity to repeat or re-produce). A minor literature writes to produce what Deleuze and Guattari refer to as a 'people to come'. Its identity is always provisional, in the process of creation. Each new text in Australian Aboriginal literature transforms what it is to be Aboriginal. A literature of minorities does not become major when there are enough examples. On the contrary, the *more* texts there are of a minor literature – the more new identities are added – the greater is the opening, becoming and *non*-recognition of those who write. The Australian Aboriginal poet, Mudrooroo (1938 –), includes all sorts of images in his poetry – other black cultures, such as the reggae of Bob Marley, *and* 'contaminating' images from Western capitalism. His work is Aboriginal, not by being a pure representation of some origin, but by creating a specific territory in which being Aboriginal is presented as a process of becoming and negotiation, incorporating and transforming images from without through its own mode of work. Such a literature would become majoritarian when its past examples are read as signs of some underlying essence: if arts councils refused funding to works for not being sufficiently Aboriginal, or if criticism discerned an underlying essence of Aboriginal literature.

ETERNAL RETURN, DIFFERENCE AND REPETITION

All 'great' literature is therefore a minor literature. Joyce's *Dubliners*, for example, allows the very style of the text to follow the voice of Dublin. But what is expressed is not something that *is*; it is not a national spirit, heritage or home. Dublin is expressed as a style and, more importantly, as a hybrid style: a mixture of religious language, slogans, phrases from romance fiction and commercial business-speak.

What makes a literature minor is not how many speakers it assembles, but the style of the assemblage. A majoritarian literature or politics presents itself as a voice above and beyond style, as a universal subject prior to any of its expressions. As an example we might take some lines from a war sonnet by Rupert Brooke (1887–1915): 'If I should die think only this of me: / That there's some corner of a foreign field / That is forever England' (Brooke 1970). Not only is *what* is expressed (or the content) identifying with a timeless homeland and a speaker who is at one with that homeland; the style is also majoritarian. There is a clear location of speaker as a distinct 'I', and a rhythm of unchallenged iambic pentameter, as though the voice were at one with an eternal English poetry. The poem repeats the past as an unchanging whole, a whole in which the speaker participates and from which he borrows his unique identity.

Great literature, as minor literature, works with a more profound repetition. It does not repeat the surface forms of literature; it does not reproduce already established forms and rhythms. What is repeated in minor literature is literary becoming. To truly repeat a Shakespeare sonnet would demand reactivating all the forces of creation that produced the original, and this may mean abandoning sonnet forms altogether. Maximum repetition is maximum difference. Repeating the past does not mean parroting its effects, but repeating the force and difference of time, producing art today that is as disruptive of the present as the art of the past. A minor literature 'repeats', not in order to express what goes before, but to express an untimely power, a power of language to disrupt identity and coherence. Joyce's *Dubliners* 'repeats' the voices of Dublin, not in order to stress their timelessness, but to disclose their fractured or machine-like quality – the way in which words and phrases become meaningless, dislocated and mutated through absolute deterritorialisation. What Joyce repeats is the power of difference.

Deleuze describes two ways of thinking about difference and repetition. On the representational model we can imagine a repeated word that is basically the same, although there will be minor and unimportant differences. This gives us the representational model of the concept. A concept enables us to see a class of things as the same, despite differences. On this model, repeating art or literature would mean copying something as faithfully as possible, trying to adhere to the model or origin. Brooke's sonnet repeats the form faithfully, and repeats the very voice of England, which precedes and grounds each of its expressions. On a positive or Deleuzean model of difference and repetition, a repeated word may look the same; but it is not sameness that produces repetition so much as difference. Each repetition of a word is always a different inauguration of that word, transforming the word's history and any context. More broadly, imagine if we were to really repeat the French Revolution. If we were to dress up in eighteenth-century costume, build a mock Bastille and re-enact the gestures, then we would only be repeating the surface form; there would be nothing revolutionary about this at all. If, however, we were to seize the revolutionary power, the demand for difference that opened the French revolution, then we would end up with something quite different, necessarily unpredictable because the first event was unpredictable. True history is anachronism. Real repetition maximises difference. When Joyce repeats the voices of Dublin they become unrecognisably different. No longer the habitual voices of everyday life that are unquestioned and unchanging, they become unstable, arbitrary and open to infinite transformation.

The two notions of difference and repetition distinguish between major and minor literatures, and the empirical and the transcendental. A minor literature repeats the past and present in order to create a future. It is a transcendental repetition: repeating the hidden forces of difference that produce texts, rather than repeating the known texts themselves. Because the voices a minor literature repeats are already not its own, it has no sense of belonging. Think of all the post-colonial texts that do not appeal to their own already given voice but repeat and transform texts of the past: Jean Rhys's (1894–1979) *Wide Sargasso Sea* (1966) 'repeats' Charlotte Brontë's (1816–55) *Jane Eyre* (1847); J. M. Coetzee's (1940–) *Foe* (1986) 'repeats' Daniel Defoe's (1661–1731) *Robinson Crusoe* (1719); Peter Carey's (1943–) *Oscar and Lucinda* (1988) 'repeats' Edmund Gosse's (1849–1928) *Father and Son* (1907); Peter Greenaway's film *Prospero's Books* (1991) 'repeats' William Shakespeare's *The Tempest* (1623). Repetition, in minor literature, repeats the voice and law of tradition in order to disclose the specific *style* of voice. We no longer see the past or law as *the* voice of, say, England, but as a voice among others, and as a power to create a future. Style, for Deleuze, is not something that ornaments voice or content. Voice, meaning or what a texts *says* is at one with its style. There is no 'message' behind literary affect and becoming; any sense of a message or an underlying meaning is an effect of specific styles. It is the mask that *produces* the effect of a speaker *behind* the mask, but one can only speak because there are masks or personae.

A majoritarian literature presents itself as the faithful description of a law or meaning independent of the text. So we *could* read any author – from Shakespeare to Joyce – as expressions of *the* great human spirit or *the* tradition. Majoritarian styles and repetitions appeal to a preceding and grounding model; they repeat what is already given with a minimum of difference. Think of all those film adaptations of eighteenth- and nineteenth-century novels that use literary voice-overs, accurate period costumes and minimise any filmic or televisual aspects. A minor literature, by contrast, does not repeat a voice or model but repeats the power of difference that produces the original. A filmic repetition of a literary work would have to transform the cinema in the same way that the literary work transformed literature. When Robert Altman filmed Raymond Carver's short stories in *Short Cuts* he did not produce a series of short films. He used the specific medium of cinema to produce overlapping but divergent narratives, and then added uniquely visual effects, such as a series of 'For Sale' signs that do not form part of the narrative, nor are they focused upon by the camera. To repeat a work of literature is not to *copy* that work, but to repeat the forces of difference that produced that work. This is a *transcendental* difference and repetition: a repetition of the virtual and hidden power of difference, and not a banal repetition of already experienced (or empirical) forms. A minor literature repeats a voice, not in order to maintain the tradition, but to transform the tradition. Rhys's *Wide Sargasso Sea* no longer allows us to read *Jane Eyre* as just a nineteenth-century novel. All the literary and cinematic transformations of *The Tempest* make the Shakespearean original different, for they disclose the power of the original *to become*.

True literature, as minor literature, is therefore an instance of Deleuze's concept of *eternal return*. The *only* thing that is repeated or returns is difference; no two moments of life can be the same. By virtue of the flow of time, any repeated event is necessarily different (even if different only to the extent that it has a predecessor). The power of life is difference and repetition, or the eternal return of difference. Each event of life transforms the whole of life, and does this over and over again. So eternity, all that is and will be, is always different from itself, always open to becoming, never at rest. Similarly, each event of literature transforms the whole of literature. It is not just that we do not read Shakespeare the same way after having read T. S. Eliot's *The Waste Land*; it is not just that we have lost the original. For the original, the texts of Shakespeare, already holds the virtual power of all later repetitions.

It is a majoritarian literature, politics and style that regards itself as representational and interpretive: as the re-presentation of an original or actual foundation which only requires interpretation or presentation through some style. A minoritarian literature, politics and style is nothing outside each of its singular events. And the repetition of *any* of these events is also a repetition of the whole. If texts like Joyce's *Dubliners* transform just what we take literature to be, then repeating Joyce would also mean repeating and reaffirming this transformative power. For Deleuze this is the eternal and untimely power of literature, or the power of eternal return. A text does not *have* a context which would limit how it might be read or what it could do. A text, if it is really literary, transforms its context, transforms the very context of literature *and* expresses the power of difference that will open up new contexts. Difference is therefore not a power *within* time; it is the power of time itself – eternal or untimely. And the only thing that does not change *through time*, the only eternal, is difference and time itself: always different.

SUMMARY

Deleuze refuses to see language as representation. There is not an inert and meaningless world that is then ordered and re-presented through signs. All life is 'semiotic', a process of creating differences that then need to be 'read' or responded to in turn. Language is one mode of the flow of life and difference. In literature we see language, not as a picture of the world but as a line of difference that produces distinct worlds. In minor literature we see language as active formation, as the creation of styles and possibilities for speakers. In its majoritarian mode, literature presents itself as the expression or representation of 'man' or a national identity. Minor literatures create collective assemblages; they form styles that allow bodies to form new territories, constantly breaking off from any image of a general or universal subject. A major literature repeats forms of the past, and subjugates itself to some supposed identity which all those forms express. A minor literature repeats nothing other than the power to be different; its becoming is not *within time* but is untimely. Difference is not the difference between different forms, or the difference from some original model; difference is the power that over and over again produces new forms.

7

BECOMING

Throughout this book you will have noticed that Deleuze's project is united by an emphasis on becoming, rather than being. But this takes quite a specific form. From the Ancient Greeks there were philosophers who argued that we only know the world through the changing flux of our sense, and that we never see things in themselves. This was why Plato rejected the second-order imitations of literature; our senses are already at one remove from what things really are, and art just presents further simulations of sense impressions. In *The Logic of Sense*, published in French in 1971, Deleuze describes his own project as an overcoming of Platonism (Deleuze 1990). Platonism is over-turned with the affirmation of becoming and simulation; there is no longer an origin or being that then becomes or goes through a process of simulation. In a reversal of Platonism we do away with the foun-dation of being, acknowledging the immanence of becoming (becoming as all there is without ground or foundation). This does not just mean *valuing* becoming over being. It means doing away with the opposition altogether. The supposed real world that would lie behind the flux of becoming is not, Deleuze insists, a stable world of being; there 'is' nothing other than the flow of becoming. All 'beings' are just relatively stable moments in a flow of becoming-life. *The* obstacle to thinking becoming, according to Deleuze, is humanism and subjectivism. Both these tendencies posit some ground for becoming: either the human as the knower of a world that becomes, or a subject that underlies becoming. Deleuze's work is an anti-humanism, not because it wants to replace the privileged image of 'man' with some other model for the emergence of life – such as culture, language or history. Deleuze's destruction of the idea of man as a foundational being is part of a more general affirmation of becoming: thought *is* becoming. (Although the word 'is' becomes problematic here, for in a world of becoming what something 'is' is always open to what it is not yet.) The task is to think without models, axioms or grounds. Philosophy, literature and science are powers of becoming. Philosophy allows us to think the forces of becoming by producing concepts of the differential or dynamic power of life; science allows us to organise matter by creating functions that allow us to extend our perception beyond what is actually given; literature allows us to become by creating affects that transform what we take experience to be.

BECOMING-IMPERCEPTIBLE

The *actual* world that we perceive is the composite of *virtual* tendencies. The colour we perceive as red and as constant is the eye's contraction (or actualisation) of light. The human eye actualises light as 'colour' but there are other beings who would actualise the flow of light in other ways: a colour-blind eye still perceives the light waves, but as monochrome. Perception, in its actual forms, therefore takes up what it can from a far more complex flow of pure difference. So there are possibilities for seeing which are virtual (flows of light), and such possibilities may or may not be actualised (or seen by an eye). So there is always more than the actual world; there are also all the potential worlds that we might see. Not only, therefore, is the actual world expanded by a virtual plane of potential, there is also a virtual dimension at the heart of any actual perception. Humans actualise sound waves by hearing music, but a bat actualises sound waves by 'seeing' and navigating. For Deleuze life begins with pure difference or becoming, or tendencies to differ – such as the differential waves of sound and light, and these differences are then actualised by different points of perception: such as the human eye. Our world of beings, the extended terms that we perceive, are contractions of flows of becoming. Furthermore, each contraction has its own duration: the human eye can perceive all the different waves of light as a block of colour, while a more complex eye or laser would not homogenise the light waves into a single colour.

To see any thing *as actual* also requires the virtual synthesis of time: we see things only by retaining the memory of past perceptions and anticipating and connecting future perceptions. I can perceive this thing *as red* only with reference to past perception, which allows me to recognise this perception as red. I can also anticipate further instances and variations of this red that are not yet present; our perceived present has this virtual halo of what is not present but is no less real. On the one hand, then, perception *reduces* difference. The human eye perceives only what interests it. We take the intense, complex and differing flows of life and perceive a world of extended material objects. On the other hand, the human eye can also expand and maximise difference: anticipating a future, recalling a past, and allowing the actual perception to be opened to the virtual. An artist, in perceiving red, might imagine all the variations and mutations that are possible but not yet actualised. Something of this is in play when we perceive *singularities*.

For the most part we do not perceive becoming; we only perceive a world as transcendent, a world of external and extended things. But it is possible, especially through art, not just to refer our sense experiences to a world of experienced things. We can also experience sensibility itself: not a sensible contracted and organised according to the specific interests of the perceiver. Deleuze refers to this as the 'being of the sensible' (Deleuze 1994). A singularity is just this becoming of the sensible, the virtual power of the sensible, its untimely possibility. Imagine walking into a room you know to be an art gallery, but the lights are off. Your eye anticipates the vision of colour that is not yet possible; without any actual colour, you already have a sense of *colour to be seen* or the potential for colour. Certain works of art can present this potential – which cannot be reduced to any actual colour – through singularity. Singularities are not images *within time* – not perceptions organised into a coherent and ordered world – they are the events from which the difference of time flows. Time, or the flow of life, is just this pulsation of sensible events or singularities, which we then experience and perceive as an actual world.

To a certain extent, then, we can think of art and its presentation of singularities as a 'becoming-imperceptible'. We become perceivable and extended bodies, or located perceivers, by *contracting* from the complex flow of life. We reduce the chaos of perceptions that we receive into an extended object, and can become 'subjects' who observe this object. By contrast, we become *imperceptible* – no longer disengaged from life and difference – by becoming one with the flow of images that is life. This is why Deleuze and Guattari favoured the literature of Kafka: stories where Kafka imagined being an insect, a burrowing animal or a machine. Here, we can imagine life from an inhuman perspective. Instead of being an image set over against the world, such as a mind that receives impressions, we recognise ourselves as nothing more than a flow of images, the brain being one image among others, one possible perception and not the origin of perceptions.

Deleuze's concept of the image ties back into his commitment to immanence and is also crucial for his creation of a concept of becoming. On a standard understanding, images or what we perceive are images *of* some *transcendent* reality. The image would be a copy of the real, a secondary or virtual 'becoming' added on to being. (There would be a world – or being – that was then perceived, or went through time and becoming, through all the images we have of it.) Deleuze, however, insists that we account for the notion of the image imma- nently. How do we come up with this idea of a mind/brain/eye that receives images? Well, we already have to have an image of the brain or self. From the flow of our experiences, movements or images we posit some organising centre, and we also posit some real world *behind* the images we see. (But we have done this *from* an immanent flow of images. In the beginning there is just an impersonal experience, which we then organise into a world set over against some 'image of thought' – the brain, mind, subject or man.) Against this notion of the image as the copy of an actual world by perceiving observers, Deleuze argues for an immanent life of imaging or simulation. A plant, for example, is not a static thing, although we perceive it as such. The plant is the reception of light, heat, moisture, insect pollination and so on; it is a process of becoming in relation to other becomings. Even more perti- nent would be the notion of an atom, which does not select or contract its perceptions but *is* nothing more than its response or reception of the forces it 'perceives'. We can think of art and philosophy as *becoming*- molecular or *becoming*-imperceptible. We do not actually want to *be* a molecule or animal, for this would mean not writing at all. But by *approaching* or imaging the inhuman point of view of animals, machines and molecules we no longer take ourselves as unchanging perceivers set over and against life. We immerse ourselves in the flow of life's perceptions. The human becomes more than itself, or expands to its highest power, not by affirming its humanity, nor by returning to animal state, but by becoming-hybrid with what is not itself. This creates 'lines of flight'; from life itself we imagine all the becomings of life, using the human power of imagination to overcome the human.

Throughout his work Deleuze uses the word 'molecular' to refer to those differences contracted by our perception. Becoming-imperceptible can be contrasted with the usual notion of theory – from the Greek *theoria*, to look – as an elevated viewpoint that disengages itself from difference and the sensible. Becoming-imperceptible is a molecular style of perception and transforms our notion of freedom. To begin with, becoming-imperceptible is the challenge of abandoning or transforming the perceived image of thought or point of view from which we judge and order life. Second, this is a molecular style of perception precisely because, freed from the human organism's interested and organising perception, perception can be opened beyond itself. Finally, this allows a new notion of freedom: not the freedom of a human self who can be disengaged from the force of life, but a freedom gained by no longer seeing ourselves as a point of view detached from life. We become free *from the human*, open to the event of becoming. Here, freedom would not be the opposite of necessity; it would not rely on a free self opposed to a necessary nature. Rather, there is a freedom in no longer seeing the world from our partial and moralising perspectives. In perceiving the force and power of life *that is also ourselves* we become with life, affirming its creative power: no longer reacting against life from a position of illusory human judgement. Freedom requires moving beyond the human to affirm life. Literature, for Deleuze, is essential here.

BECOMING-LITERATURE

Consider, for example, the fiction of Brett Easton Ellis, especially a work of extreme violence such as *American Psycho* (1991). This is a novel about a yuppie who devours videos, designer labels, fads, popular culture and high-class restaurants. He also has a voracious appetite for torture and destruction: killing and consuming the bodies of women, vagrants, blacks and children. One way to read this book would be to say that it is 'about evil'. 'We' could read it as the faithful description of the mind-set of 'the' serial killer. Further, it could be read as an indictment of capitalism, corporatism, America, commodity culture or modernity. This is just the sort of reading Deleuze and Guattari question; for capitalism is not just a moment *within history*; it is a tendency of all social life. It is the very nature of any political space to produce exchange, system and 'inhuman' structures. To read *American Psycho* as the description of a *specific* and *located* evil (whether that be male violence, capitalism or just the pathology of the killer) would be a *moral* reading. It would require a point of view outside the text, such that 'we' could adopt a separate position of critique and judgement.

From a Deleuzean point of view, though, this type of reading would present us with the problem of all theory and moralism: how can this judging system of values justify itself? Only if it perceives itself as separate, stable and disengaged from what it perceives can the judging eye accuse a character of evil. The problem with any moral system of good and evil is that it takes what is essentially an *active* selection – 'I affirm this, I reject that' – and presents it *reactively*, as already determined through a system of immutable values – 'this *is* evil'. What literature, especially texts like *American Psycho*, does is to decompose the *finite* positions of moralism. It expands perception beyond the located point of view of moral judgement. It perceives *ethically*: it perceives the 'ethos' or place of habit *from which* specific characters and actions emerge. In *American Psycho* the central character is formed from the first-person narration of restaurant menus, chat-show topics, designer trends and trendy slang; he is not so much a located person as a series of investments and intensities. Sections of the novel are nothing more than seemingly 'straight' reviews – in music mag style – of 1980s music, with no sense of personal character or psychology.

Becoming-imperceptible means no longer knowing who or what we are; it means seeing with greater openness the differences, intensities and singularities that traverse us. *American Psycho*, for example, cannot draw a clear boundary between good and evil. The same forces that compose the serial killer – the blaming condemnation of the welfare state, the desire for increased visceral intensity in the face of commercial banality and the investment in the autonomous, isolated and controlling body – are also those that compose 'normal' America. Deleuze and Guattari write of the power to recognise the 'micro-fascisms' in us all: the tendency for reactionary investments, regardless of our revolutionary interests (Deleuze and Guattari 1983). *American Psycho* diagnoses the reactionary investments that cannot be contained within a character. The narration will repeat the 'dissection' style of 1980s restaurant menus, which describe animal parts, sauces and accompaniments with tireless detail, with the same tone that later describes the sexuality and torture of bodies. The narration moves from an inclusive 'we', mentioning all the values, images, pop-song lyrics and brand-names that make up our life, to a pathological, violent and destructive psychosis. In one scene the text moves from the standard, clichéd and erotic description of a sex-scene to yet one more, now thoroughly banal, description of mutilation and torture. The literary art of *American Psycho* is the 'becoming-imperceptible' of its style. We never have a sense of *who* is speaking, no sense of a delimited narrator. The central character, Bateman, is nothing more than the styles, labels and trends he quotes. We do not view the serial killer from some disengaged viewpoint; in reading we perceive the intensities and investments that are *at one and the same time* those of a violent evil and those of 'our' world.

Everyday moral narratives, such as fables, parables and soap-operas, operate with the fixed terms of good and evil, and do so from a shared point of view of common sense and human recognition. Literature destroys this border between perceiver and perceived. We are no longer placed in a position of ordering judgement but *become other* through a confrontation with the forces that compose us. This is freedom: not a freedom to judge which comes from knowing who we are, but a liberation from our finite self-images, an opening to life. At its simplest level we can see how ethical becoming or freedom is limited by a fixed image of thought. If we accept who we are and what we should be, then we can simply exclude those who are 'evil'; we can remain good, holy and 'pure' from the forces that supposedly work against life. Alternatively, we can demand a perception of *impersonal* joy and sadness. Here we affirm what increases our power to become (joy) and only say 'no' to what limits us (sadness). The power we affirm through joy is the power of a life beyond our specific self. (If I affirm my actions as part of the women's movement then I expand the power of the whole of life; this is because such affirmations aim to include, expand and create relations. If, by contrast, I assert my power as a killer, rapist or judgemental moralist, then I diminish the forces of the life and lives that lie beyond me; this is because I do not recognise those powers beyond me; I reinforce, rather, than expand, my perceptual boundaries.) Against good and evil, as moral opposites,

Deleuze follows Spinoza in arguing for an ethical relation between joy and sadness. Sad perceptions are those which diminish my power, and the power of all life; in joy I perceive what is not myself and in so doing expand who I am and what I might become.

There would be sadness, of course, in the image of the serial killer in *American Psycho*, the sadness of a being who can only devour other bodies and who cannot respond to all the perceptions or worlds opened by other persons. But there would also be a sadness in the moralising observer or reader who saw the evil of another as simply 'evil', as simply opposed to one's own innocent life. Far from moralising condemnation, Deleuze suggests that we gain an adequate idea of the inhuman forces that produce sadness. This means *not* seeing evil as located within characters but recognising the desires and investments that turn life against itself. In the case of *American Psycho* we see the serial killer figure of Bateman as composed of images and investments which are never simply his and never entirely other than ourselves. His violence and frenzied self-investment comes from an investment in the hardened American individual. His gym-cultivated body, his desperate attempt to experience a highly individualised intensity, and his language of self-promotion are not so much personal features added on to his character as they are impersonal forces from which his character is effected. *American Psycho* is the diagnosis or 'symptomatology' of a collection of investments. In reading we 'become imperceptible', not by judging characters, but by experiencing the forces of life from which judgements of good and evil are derived. Becoming-imperceptible is not something that can be achieved once and for all; it is a becoming, not a being. It is the challenge of freedom and perception: of opening ourselves to the life that passes through us, rather than objectifying that life in advance through a system of good and evil.

BECOMING-ANIMAL

Becoming-imperceptible is the *Idea* (the limit or infinite expansion) of perception. If we take the power of perception to its 'nth power' we would respond to all possible differences, and to be so sensitive to difference would demand that we were no longer beings *who perceived*. We would become one with the differential flows of life. Becoming-imperceptible is the challenge of no longer acting as a separate and selecting point within the perceived world, but of becoming different with, and through, what is perceived. One way to think becoming-other than the perceived image of 'man' is through becoming-animal. Becoming animal does not mean becoming *like* an animal, or *being* an animal and leaving the terrain of the human altogether. It is a *becoming*-animal and not a *being*-animal because it is hybrid. We begin from what is not animal, neither animal nor human but 'transversal'.

Deleuze and Guattari cite Ahab's fascination for the whale in Herman Melville's (1819–91) great nineteenth-century novel, *Moby Dick*. Ahab pursues the whale, not for any end or purpose, and certainly not to assert his power *over* the whale. Rather, becoming-animal is the power, not to conquer what is other than the self, but to transform oneself in perceiving difference (Deleuze and Guattari 1987: 243). As the novel progresses Ahab acts, not for any external reason or end; his actions are immediately prompted by the strange life of the whale. And the whale is perceived in its singularity: not as a symbol or metaphor for life. It must be *this* whale that captivates Ahab; the whale is perceived as a singular event of life with its own power to become. The novel is about transversal becoming: neither the becoming *of* 'man' (Ahab) nor the becoming *of* nature (where the whale would represent life in general). It expresses two distinct becomings – Ahab's perceiving fascination and the whale's mobile body. The narrative is made up of the events that come about through the combination of these becomings, events intended neither by Ahab nor the whale.

For Deleuze, transversal becomings are the key to the openness of life. Life is not composed of pre-given forms that simply evolve to become what they are, as though becoming could be attributed to the becoming *of* some being. Because there is always more than one line or tendency of becoming – say, the animal and the human – it is possible for intersections or encounters to produce unheard of lines of new becoming, or 'lines of flight'. A gene or virus that develops one way in one species would mutate differently in another. What it *is* depends on the life it encounters. A being is just its power for such multiple becomings. We enhance our life or power by 'mutating' or 'varying' in as many ways as possible, through a maximum of encounters. We limit our life by restricting our becomings (through pre-given moral codes or norms). The human may have its own tendencies of becoming (such as consciousness, memory, writing and so on) but it can also expand its perception to encounter other becomings, such as becoming-animal.

INTERPRETOSIS

Deleuze and Guattari explore this idea of becoming-animal *against* Freud and through Kafka. They regard a certain tradition of Freudian psycho-analysis as typical of 'interpretosis': a Western disease that traces all becomings back to some origin. First, they oppose the idea of the animal as a representation or a sign to be interpreted. In Freud's case of the wolf-man, Freud takes his patient's fascination with wolves back to a childhood memory. By a series of associations Freud argues that the memories lead back to a 'primal scene' where the patient, as a child, had witnessed his parents having sexual intercourse with his father 'mounting' his mother from behind. The child therefore represents his father with a wolf figure. Freud traces all connections back to this child-hood trauma; he even interprets the 'W' of 'wolf as a sign of the bent-over servant girl who, in turn, symbolises the sexual position of his mother. The rear and legs form the image of an inverted 'W'. This is what Freud refers to as 'overdetermination' where a complex series of different affects all lead back, through different memories and time-scales, to an original parental fantasy. For Freud, then, the wolf and the patient's fascination are signifiers of the original alienation all humans must feel, as cast out from their maternal origin.

This 'interpretosis' is not unique to Freud and is typical, Deleuze argues, of the Western representational schema, whereby every ex-perienced affect is *read* as the signifier *of* some original scene. Desire, also, is interpreted as a desire for a lost origin that is then displaced or repressed through substitutions and images. In contrast with this negativity of the image (where the image is always referred back to an event that is its external cause), Deleuze and Guattari argue for the internal intensity of affects. It is the image itself that is desirable and affective, and not some concealed 'belief' or meaning. Deleuze and Guattari use the idea of 'becoming-animal' to describe the posi-tivity and multiplicity of desire and affect. The child's fascination for the wolf is not for what the wolf *represents* but for the wolf's entirely different mode of becoming: wolves travel in packs, at night, wandering. There is a desire here that is directed to a multiplicity of affects (all that the wolf does and can do and that is not attached to any single wolf character so much as a collection or 'swarm'). This is a desire, not for what the wolf *is* or symbolises, but for potential actions. Also, and most importantly, this desire is not for what one *lacks*; the wolf does not stand in for that original scene of trauma where the child loses his mother to his father. The desire directed to the wolf is not one of possessing or regaining some object towards which desire is directed; it is a desire to expand or become-other through what is more than oneself. The wolf is not a signifier of some human quality or figure; it is another mode of perception or becoming. In perceiving the wolf we perceive differently, no longer separated from the world in the human point of view.

For Deleuze and Guattari, then, becoming-animal is not just an issue within psychoanalysis. It offers a new way of thinking about perceiving and becoming. Freud had regarded the patient's world as interpretable or 'overcoded', with all experiences leading back to a scene of loss, trauma or separation from the maternal source of life. Human becoming could always be interpreted from the point of view of the oedipal drama. Human life, says Freud, aims for its own death or a return to an earlier state of things: an imagined point before all desire and difference. Against this, Deleuze and Guattari take becoming-animal as evidence of the positivity of desire, the tendency of perception to become through what is not itself rather than always retrieving some lost, mythical and originally unified image of itself. Whereas most theories of desire imagine desire as directed towards possessing what one lacks or has lost, or as directed to what lies beyond life, Deleuze and Guattari do not set desire against life. Life is desire, and desire is the expansion of life through creation and transformation. Becoming-animal is, therefore, not a being or having. In becoming-animal you do not wear a cat-suit or imagine humans and animals as equal members of some grand ecological community where 'we' are all the same. What draws perception to the animal is not empathy but *anomaly*. It is the non-familial, non-individual (or pack-like) wandering of the wolves which attracts the wolf-man.

Becoming-animal shows that becoming is not a series of actions directed towards some image that we hope to replicate; it is a trans-formation at each point of action with no external end. To understand this mode of becoming we can turn to Deleuze's early example of the swimmer in *Difference and Repetition*. If I try to learn to swim by mechanically copying the instructor's movements as they are demonstrated out of the water then I will never learn the art of swimming. (I will never learn to compose music if I just repeat the sonatas of Beethoven. We will never do philosophy if we just repeat learned arguments.) I will only learn to swim if I see what the instructor does not as a self-contained action but as a creative *response*. I do not repeat his arm movements; I repeat the sense of the water or feel for the waves that produces his arm movements. My arms need to feel the water and become in the way a swimmer's arms become. Because my body is different – female – this might mean that a *faithful repetition* of his swimming might require slightly different arm movements. I have to feel what good swimming *does*, not what it *is*. I have to feel how a swimmer acts, rather than literally copying these movements. (Similarly, composing in the manner of a great composer would mean feeling the inventive force at the heart of Beethoven's sonatas. Producing great philosophy would require feeling the force of a problem, not repeating all the answers.) Becoming, in its true force, is not bounded by what has already become or is actualised, but it is spurred on by perceiving the virtual powers that are expressed in actions.

Becoming-animal is not, then, attaining the state of what the animal *means* (the supposed strength or innocence of animals); nor is it becoming what the animal *is*. It is not behaving like an animal. Becoming-animal is a feel for the animal's movements, perceptions and becomings: imagine seeing the world as if one were a dog, a beetle or a mole.

BECOMING-ANIMAL AND LITERATURE

This brings us to the connection between becoming-animal and literature. Becoming-animal has been expressed, most notably, in works by Kafka and Melville. But this is not just a particular type of literature. It expresses a power of literature: the power to perceive differently by tearing perception from its human home. It is significant that Deleuze and Guattari refer both to Kafka and Melville. In *Moby Dick* Ahab's fascination for the whale is a becoming precisely because Ahab is drawn to the *anomalous* character of the whale. The whale, Moby Dick, is a true becoming, having wandered away from the fleet of whales; his whiteness, his destructive power and his separation all complicate any perception of what the whale *is*. Early on in Melville's novel, before the passage of Ahab towards the whale, we are presented with a taxonomy of whale classification, an exhaustive study of the whale species. But Moby Dick and Ahab's fascination present themselves as affects irreducible to such attempts at meaning and interpretation. It is the elusiveness of the whale, its resistance to sense and comprehension, that leads Ahab out of his human and interested ventures – whale-hunting for profit or sea-faring – into a senseless search for *this* particular whale.

Becoming-animal is the power of literature to present percepts and affects freed from their moorings in the drama of human interests. *Moby Dick can* (and has) been read as a novel about the search for human meaning, such that Ahab imagines that if only he conquers Moby Dick he will achieve integrity, sense and order. (The whale becomes a 'floating signifier', representative of what stands in the way of ultimate meaning or comprehension.) Deleuze and Guattari typically read literature against such manifestly interpretive (or hermeneutic) methods. Indeed, they select just those authors, such as Kafka and Melville, who have been read as producing the image or sign of a meaning that lies forever out of reach. Instead of reading literature as a quest for meaning and interpretation, Deleuze and Guattari argue that literature shows that literature is about affects and intensities. It is only the reactive literary critic who wants to interpret Melville's whale and Kafka's insect as 'signifiers' of some ultimate meaning. It is always possible to read literature as an art of recognition, as about 'ourselves' and 'the' human search for meaning. This art of interpretation or hermeneutics requires that we 'overcode' literature, seeing each text as an expression or representation of some underlying meaning (a meaning that is the same throughout history, the drama of 'man's' search for sense). Alternatively, literature can be read for what it produces, for its transformations. Instead of reading the 'animals' of literature as symbols – what do they mean? – we can see the animal as a possible opening for new styles of perception. In this case, becoming-animal would indicate a tendency in literature, and art, of rending perception open to what is not itself. Literature would not be about the expression of meaning but the *production* of sense, allowing new perceptions and new worlds.

To make this more clear we can look at Deleuze and Guattari's work on Kafka. Of all authors Kafka is often read as *the* author of negativity. (Deleuze and Guattari do, though, read most literature and philosophy against the industry standard. They seem to be saying that if even Kafka can be read as a literature of positive becoming, then all literature *can* be read affirmatively. Why would we want to posit some ultimate meaning *behind* a text, if a text can be opened to what it does?) Kafka's *The Trial* (1925), for example, is usually read as an allegory of the law. The main character wanders through passage after passage never arriving at the law. On the negative and traditional reading we can see the law as what must always remain hidden; we can only produce images and interpretations of the law, never the law itself. We have an idea of the law – of a justice or good beyond conception or measure – but any attempt to represent or articulate this law defiles its essential purity. On this reading, we are essentially alienated and guilty, and Kafka's fictions are symbols of this alienation, our loss of any sense of a present or presentable God or law. Kafka's great story, 'Metamorphosis', where Gregor Samsa awakens to find himself transformed into a beetle would be a symbol or allegory of the inhumanity, alienation or displacement at the heart of all finite human life.

Deleuze and Guattari, however, read Kafka's work, not as an allegory that represents a law that is forever 'other' or transcendent. On the contrary, they argue, the wanderings in Kafka's texts are positive. There is an intensity or enjoyment of movement itself, of opening doorway after doorway, of crossing space, or burrowing or playing the insect. In fact, the 'law' as supposed end or reason for this movement is produced *from* the movement. Kafka's texts produce doorways, passages, animal movements and images, all with no law or fulfilment lying behind them. Law or meaning is exposed as an *effect* of action, and not as some ultimate goal or origin which drives action. It is the disease of interpretation that imposes a law: if you were wandering from door to door then you must have been searching for some end; if you were transformed into an insect then you must have *lost* your humanity. We could read Kafka's story, 'The Hunger-Artist', as an image of submission, a man who decides to starve himself in order to inflict punishment upon himself precisely because any law will always be out of reach, always cruel and arbitrary. Following Deleuze and Guattari, though, this self-starvation can be read as variation, experimentation. Against reading Kafka's becomings and animals as symbols for a life that forever remains enigmatic and alien, Deleuze and Guattari see Kafka's literature as a production of new intensities. The beetle, the mole, the hunger-artist and the castle do not *mean* anything; they produce new styles of perception. See the world as an animal, as a series of passages going nowhere, or from the point of view of a diminishing body. The fascination for the animal is a fascination for the world seen, not from an already organised position of opinion, but seen anew.

BECOMING-WOMAN

In his cinema books and in *A Thousand Plateaus* Deleuze grants becoming-woman a privileged position. According to Deleuze and Guattari all becomings begin and pass through becoming-woman. There are two reasons for this claim. The first has to do with their argument that there can be no becoming-man because man is essentially majoritarian. The second reason has to do with with Deleuze and Guattari's reinterpretation of the psychoanalytic understanding of sexuality. We will deal first with the argument regarding becoming-man.

There can be no becoming-man precisely because man is not just one extended being among others within the world. Man is the subject: the point of view or ground from which all other beings or becomings are supposedly determined. It is the very concept of man that underpins the logic of transcendence. Only with some privileged being as the centre for all experience can there be a strict distinction between the 'inner' life of mind or consciousness and the outside world viewed or represented by mind. Man is 'majoritarian' not because he outnumbers other beings, but because *any* being can be included within the measure of man. In the idea of multiculturalism, for example, it is often assumed that we ought to allow for plural cultural differences because deep down we are all members of the family of man. Racism, for Deleuze and Guattari, is not a logic of exclusion; its violence and tyranny lies in inclusion. What explicit and insidious racisms share is the standard of man. For the conventional racist the other is 'inhuman', but for the moralist the other is human, 'just like me'. We are all white and western. We are all the same; other cultures need only to be recognised as just like 'us'.

It is the very concept of man that has impeded us from thinking the active and affirmative difference of life. It is the concept of man that has both set us against a world of appearances, and devalued those appearances as 'only' appearances. We need to see the world, Deleuze argues, not as some thing that 'we' know through perceptions, but as a plane of impersonal perceptions. Man, as the subject, has always functioned as that point of stable being or identity which somehow must come to know or perceive an outside world. This is so even when 'man' is interpreted as historical or cultural, for even here history and culture are regarded as the becoming *of* man.

In order to think becoming positively, therefore, we need to think beyond the logic of man. If, however, we were to simply add another *being* to this logic, such as woman, we would still be within the same logic of the subject: a logic that posits a ground from which becoming is determined. To think other than man requires that we think *other than being*: not a world that *is* and that only needs to be perceived and represented, but a world of difference and becoming, with no point of that difference being privileged over any other. What is other than *man-as-being* is becoming-woman. We could not say that there *is* an other of man. This would fall back into a logic of distinct beings; we can only become other, becoming other than being, become other than man: become-woman.

ANTI-OEDIPUS: THE ATTACK ON FREUD

The first reason for the privileged status of becoming-woman is that woman is the opening away from the closed image of man; if there is another mode of becoming then becoming lacks any single ground or subject. The second reason for the importance of becoming-woman has to do with the impersonal and unbounded nature of sexual desire. Deleuze and Guattari offer a radically new and anti-humanist account of sexual difference, and this insistence on the *inhuman* character of sexuality goes back to Deleuze's *Difference and Repetition*. Deleuze begins by agreeing in part with Freud's transformation of the notion of sexuality. Freud argues that sexuality is libido, a free-floating energy that comes to be organised through *investments*. For Freud, there are certain drives for life – such as the need for food and warmth – but these become *sexual* when we desire what is *more* than life: when the child enjoys the sucking of the breast or nipple, regardless of whether it provides nourishment. (That is, we are not born with a sexual orientation but have to form objects of desire. We become who we are, sexually, by developing preferred pathways for our desire that are not reducible to the needs of life.) Libido begins without any objects; it is just the drive of the organism for self-preservation and the *reduction* of tensions (such as hunger, thirst, cold). Sexuality occurs through the organisation and deflection of libido. The libido is organised, for example, when the child's mouth expects and re-finds satisfaction at the mother's breast; deflection occurs when the child enjoys 'sucking' even in the absence of the breast. The first *sexual* object is not the actual breast providing food, but the *virtual fantasised* breast, which is the image of remembered enjoyment.

Following Freud, Deleuze begins from the notion of a free-floating desire or libido: not free-floating in the sense of amorphous and undifferentiated but not restricted to particular objects or fulfilments. But Deleuze also makes two crucial departures from Freud and psychoanalysis. First, he criticises Freud for *personalising* desire or reducing it to a familial model. Freud's explanation of desire begins from the relation between mother and child. According to Deleuze, though, the fixed terms of 'mother' and 'child' are only formed after desire has been organised and socialised. We need the modern notion of family, for example, to think of the first life relation as a mother–child relation; and we can only have the mother–father figures of the family after a long history of passing from tribes, to extended clans, to modern nuclear units. The mother–child dyad is not the beginning of desire, for desire begins collectively. The individual or solitary child is the culmination of a history leading from collections of tribal bodies to the modern isolated body. Desire, for Deleuze, does not begin *from* a relation between persons – such as the mother and child with the intervening father. Desire begins impersonally and collectively, and from a multiplicity of investments which traverse persons. Body-parts are invested *before* persons. The mouth finds the breast, but this breast is not a signifier of the mother. Furthermore, before the *private* investment in organs (such as the attachment of the breast to the 'mother') there is a collective investment: the tribe that elevates the breast or 'womb' of the earth. When the figure of the mother eventually emerges she is a contraction of all these historical and political investments. We need only look at modern advertising to see how motherhood is still invested through figures of nature, and even religious resonances of the Madonna or earth goddess. Desire, for Deleuze, is not to be reduced to sexual relations between persons. On the contrary, 'persons' are formed through the organisation of desire. I become a body through a relation to other bodies, eventually investing, perhaps, in an image of myself as an enclosed ego.

The crucial challenge of Deleuze's theory of desire, against psychoanalysis and against common sense is the idea that life and desire do not begin from bounded organisms. There is a flow of life or genetic material, the 'intense germinal influx', which passes through and across bodies. In its original and differential power life is not organised into bodies; bodies are formed from investments, or from the active and ongoing interactions of becomings. I do, however, think of myself as a closed and autonomous being, bounded by death: but this is because of a long history in which we have invested in the organised and enclosed human individual. The problem with Freudian psychoanalysis, for Deleuze and Guattari, is that it begins its analysis from the bounded individual or ego, rather than explaining the political and social emergence of the ego. For Freud, the aim of life is for all organisms to return to their original quiescent state, prior to the disruption of desire. For Deleuze, though, life has no original closed state. Life does not begin from the bounded organism but from flows.

This brings us to the second transformation of the notion of sexuality and becoming-woman. Not only is desire pre-personal, beginning from connections between body-parts; desire is also pre-human. Life, we have said, is a flow of desire. Human beings, as *extended bodies* who recognise themselves as subjects, must repress the flow or genesis that passes through them. We repress, then, not because there are objects that are denied us; we do not repress because we have to renounce the mother's body. We repress because of the *excess* of life; we are always more than the closed image of the self we take ourselves to be. The forces of life exceed the simple actual bodies we perceive; we repress the excess, violence and disruption of life – the creative force that transgresses the boundaries of persons or intentions. We tend to think of sexuality as something 'we' do, as a relation between humans. But human bodies, for Deleuze, are effects of a sexual becoming, vehicles rather than agents of life. The image we have of the child who must repress his desire for his mother in order to identify with the social image of his father represses a more radical and *revolutionary* desire and sexuality. To explain desire as originally desire *of* the child *for* the (impossible/prohibited) mother produces an image of man as that being who can originate and explain his own sexuality. Sexuality, desire and becoming are interpreted as human: as a relation between man and his biological origin. Against this explanation of desire *from* bodies, Deleuze describes a desire that produces and exceeds bodies. Desire is free flow, creative difference and becoming. (So Deleuze also rejects anything like a 'selfish gene' theory which would argue that genes strive to maintain survival regardless of our intentions; for there is no 'end' or goal to variation. The gene is not 'selfish' but radically variant, for variation's own sake. It is difference, not selfishness, which is the drive of life.)

For Deleuze and Guattari a true politics needs to think sexual flow, becoming and difference *anti-oedipally*: against the idea of a child who represses its desire for its mother and becomes just like its father. Anti-oedipal desire is an 'orphan': it has no original identity or home. Western thought, Deleuze and Guattari argue, is built on the idea of the prohibition of incest, on the idea that we must *renounce* our desire for our mother in order to become social and human. Woman, therefore, is produced as an impossible, lost and prohibited origin – as what must be repressed and excluded in order for human history to begin. Deleuze and Guattari therefore regard becoming-woman as the opening for a new understanding of desire that does not begin with the loss or repression of an original object. Desire is a flow of connection, production and ever more complex differentiation. It is the 'story' of incest that represses this radical desire and tells us what we must have wanted. By prohibiting incest society *produces the mother* as a denied object and creates a law that is other than life; it turns the power of life against life. Politics begins from the image of 'man' as other than woman, as the being capable of renouncing biological life for cultural ends. 'Man' is therefore produced through the repression and prohibition of woman. The prohibition produces the law and the bodies regulated by the law. The law begins with force and punishment, and bodies are effects of this cruel law.

A radical politics, for Deleuze and Guattari, will begin from a desire that is not the desire *of* man, and will not assume the closed human body as a basic political unit. Rather, through art and literature we can look at all those investments and images that have produced 'man' as the transcendent body and value that organises the political. Thinking a desire beyond the prohibition of woman, thinking a desire that traverses the human body, means thinking of the becoming of woman, not as *a* sex but as the opening to 'a thousand tiny sexes'. Becoming-woman is therefore the opening of a desire that is pre-personal, anti-oedipal and directly revolutionary. It is not a desire explained from within the story of man or human history. It is a desire radically other than man and his negation of life. Desire has been repressed by the image of 'man' as a being whose desire is essentially forbidden. For this reason Deleuze and Guattari also tie becoming-woman to the impulse of literature.

BECOMING-WOMAN AND LITERATURE

Deleuze and Guattari reverse the Freudian (and interpretive) use of myth and literature. Freud read the Greek tragedy of *Oedipus* as a sign of an underlying human drama. Oedipus is depicted as unwittingly killing his father and marrying his mother; and the drama has so much power, according to Freud, because it represents a universal human desire. Freud then saw all dreams, fantasies and other acts of literature as versions of this myth. The unconscious, for Freud, merely re-told this story in ever-varying forms. The unconscious, then, functioned as a personal and timeless 'theatre', replaying the oedipal drama within us all. For Deleuze and Guattari, the unconscious, far from being mythic and representational or something to be interpreted, is social, political and productive. (What is unconscious are not 'my' desires, but the history and politics of investments and energies from which 'I' am effected.) The unconscious produces all sorts of bizarre connections, investments and images – such as the wolf-man's fascination with wolves, the child's intense interest in machines, the artist's commitment to colour, or the drug addict's addiction to hallucinations. It is the psychoanalyst who *decodes* these productions and connections as signifiers of the human oedipal drama. The wolf becomes the father, the hallucinations a recompense for desire lost and the child's toy a substitution for the mother's body. For Deleuze and Guattari, Freud's mistake was to see the oedipal drama as a representation, rather than a *creation*, of an image of desire. The Greek play produces a connection between desire for the mother (the queen Jocasta) and the death of the father; and the mother–father figures in this drama are directly political: a king and a queen. The tragedy is not an image of the timeless modern family; the family has been produced from the history of such dramas and investments.

Deleuze and Guattari therefore follow Nietzsche, rather than Freud, in arguing for the *political* and not personal nature of the unconscious. Events like Greek tragedy may, they admit, produce investments – such as the image of the desired queen who is also Oedipus's mother. But *Oedipus* is not a drama about 'the' human family; it is about a specific king and political power. The modern notion of the 'father' is developed *from* these collective and political investments; for Deleuze, the modern father is derived from the invested image in the male political leader. Before there is a personal and private image of 'man' or the 'father', social machines (through events such as Greek tragedy) invest in images of the king, the despot, the banker, the cop or the fascist. 'Man' is produced from social roles; and such social investments have to be created in collective spectacle: in everything from rituals of torture to modern cinema and popular literature. This means that literature is *productive*, not representative. Literature has the power to mobilise desire, to create new pre-personal investments, and enables thought and affects that extend beyond the human. Literature is the power of becoming beyond any already given 'image of thought' or any rule of art. Becoming-woman, or the destruction of oedipal man, through literature is the very opening of the political and the future. Literature transforms the political space from a relation 'among men' to the production of inhuman affects and intensities. The human is no longer a site of recognition within which we communicate; the human is the effect of a communication or transmission of 'pre-personal singularities' across a plane of becoming. Literature is, therefore, not a vehicle for veiling and representing unconscious and timeless dramas. Literature produces new dramas and intensities. Literature is not reducible to the story and explanation of man; it always possesses the power to move beyond man: becoming-woman.

SUMMARY

We often think of becoming as something that a being does or goes through. Deleuze reverses this relation. There are becomings, such as actions, perceptions, variations and so on; from this flux of becomings we perceive or organise beings. We also tend to think of becoming and action as directed towards some end or goal, so that we become or act in order to be 'human' or moral. Deleuze argues that true becoming does not have an end outside itself. So, becoming-animal does not mean acting *in order to* impersonate or *be* like an animal; it means changing and varying in inhuman (animal) ways without any sense of pre-given purpose or goal. 'Man', traditionally, has always represented an end or goal of life, such that we act in order to fulfil our humanity. By contrast, Deleuze insists that we value action and becoming itself, freed from any human norm or end. This is why becoming begins with becoming-woman, becoming other than man. Finally, literature can be seen as a becoming-woman, for in literature we no longer see language as the representation of some underlying human norm, but as the creation and exploration of new styles of perception and becoming.

AFTER DELEUZE

There are three main areas where Deleuze's philosophy has been of influence: film theory, political theory and feminist theory. In *The Cinematic Body* the film theorist, Steven Shaviro (1993), uses Deleuze's cinema works to argue for a directly affective approach to film. Instead of watching films as disengaged spectators who then interpret the meaning or narrative, Shaviro argues that cinema can have quite physiological and visceral effects on the eye. The content of film is neither cognitive nor representational – so the visual is not the sign of some underlying sense. (Think of the violent light or cuts in films, such as *Bladerunner*, that do not represent reality so much as produce effects of simulation and unreality.) Cinema operates by direct affect and disrupts the identity of the viewer: 'Perception has become unconscious. It is neither spontaneously active nor freely receptive, but radically passive, the suffering of a violence perpetrated against the eye' (Shaviro 1993: 51). D. N. Rodowick has also written a quite complex work on Deleuze's philosophy of time and cinema which focuses on the concept of the 'time-image' and the challenge that 'irrational cuts' in film make to the synthesising power of the eye (Rodowick (1997). Perhaps the most radical dimension in Deleuze's visual theory is his concept of affect, which is not so much what *we* see but refers to the power of images themselves. Brian Massumi has pushed this idea beyond Deleuze to look at the ways in which images can have affect well beyond the subject. He cites the television images of the former US president Ronald Reagan in which the vague and shaky voice and physique did not so much send a message or meaning as lull the viewer's body and response into non-objection (Massumi 1996). Massumi has taken Deleuze's approach to images well beyond Deleuze, exploring all the ways in which politics operates through, and produces, the affects of power and the power of affects. Massumi's most recent work is *A Shock to Thought*, and is not so much a book *on* Deleuze and politics as it is a book on politics *after* Deleuze (Massumi 2001).

In political theory Deleuze's work has been used to criticise the notion of the State. Recall that for Deleuze *the* illusion of thought is transcendence; we act, think and imagine but then become enslaved to forms that we have created from action. Radical thinking requires a liberation from the laws and norms that seem to govern thought from outside. For film and literature this means that we need to see works as *productive* of meaning, and not as expressive of some pre-given 'message'. For political theory this means seeing classes, states and identities as results of active and *ongoing* creation, and not as norms or laws which we ought to fulfil or obey. Michael Hardt, who also wrote a book on Deleuze's philosophy (Hardt 1993), has teamed up with the Italian philosopher Antonio Negri (who also wrote works with Guattari) to form a new political theory of praxis (Hardt and Negri 1994). Here, they argue, we should not think of politics as the relation among fixed organisations or *constituted* powers (such as the State or classes), we need to think politics as living labour in praxis, as constituting itself through work and social relations. The State is not some law that we need to impose on our life to regulate our behaviour; we should think politics beyond the State-form. Politics would be a constant act of creation through collective labour and action. No pre-given unit or norm – neither the State, nor man, nor the 'worker' – should act as some ground for praxis. A related but significant development in Deleuze and political theory has been articulated by the Australian philosopher, Paul Patton, who argues that Deleuze's philosophy enables an *active* approach to politics. Patton uses the notion of 'minoritarian' to criticise colonialist models of power. Indigenous populations (such as those of Canada and Australia) should not be considered through, nor included within, the norms of property owning white majoritites. Their claims to land and identity are not demands to recognise some pre-existing essence or group. It is in the political act of claiming and expressing new relations to the earth that such groups both disrupt the majority standard and open up to new futures (Patton 2000). Patton refers to a 'becoming-indigenous of the social imaginary' whereby new political concepts could be created through the encounters with previously excluded cultures (Patton 2000: 126). The work of Hardt and Negri and Patton is a specifically Deleuzean extension of the rereading of Spinoza for politics. Deleuze insisted on the immanence of Spinoza for ethics and politics, such that social norms and laws should be seen as active creations of the living multitude. Just as Deleuze reread the work of Spinoza in order to argue for an immanent and creative philosophy, so two feminist philosophers have also reread Spinoza (in part through Deleuze) in order to argue for the central role of the imagination in sexual politics. One's identity is not one's own but is formed through our perception of others and of the political whole. There can be active imaginations – say, if I imagine a political whole or culture capable of creating and affirming difference – and reactive imaginings – say, if the white male body of reason becomes *the* norm for the political body. This emphasis on political creation has been artfully explored in the work of Moira Gatens and Genevieve Lloyd, whose recent book on Spinoza stresses the political import of the imagination and follows Deleuze's affirmative reading of the philosophical tradition (Gatens and Lloyd 1999).

Feminist theory has also used Deleuze's work to challenge the idea that politics needs to appeal to identities in order to criticise the dominant order. In its early days Deleuze was criticised for dissolving sexual difference into an inhuman flux, but those same feminists who criticised Deleuze are now rallying to his defence. Rosi Braidotti argues for 'nomadic subjects': bodies who form multiple identities through various actions and interventions. The idea that one *is* woman, white, middle class, and so on, is not a question of being, but the result of engagements with other bodies and other events of political difference (Braidotti 1994). For Elizabeth Grosz, Deleuze's work provides a way of rethinking bodies beyond the male–female binary. The very borders or outlines of the body, Grosz argues, are produced through relations to a malleable outside. The inside–outside border of the body – in its relation to the world and others – is not given once and for all but is an ongoing production and creation (Grosz 1994).

Deleuze's work on literature – his books on Proust, Sacher-Masoch and Kafka and his frequent literary references – are frequently mentioned in books about Deleuze. But the consequences for Deleuze and literary studies have yet to be spelled out with the degree of intensity that characterises film, political and feminist theory. There have been two book length studies of Deleuze in relation to specific authors: Eugene Holland's *Baudelaire and Schizoanalysis* (1993) and John Hughes's *Lines of Flight: Reading Deleuze with Hardy, Gissing, Conrad, Woolf* (1997). As yet, though, there is not a 'Deleuzean' movement in literary criticism: there is no equivalent to Jacques Derrida's creation of deconstruction, Michel Foucault's influence on New Historicism or Freud's psychoanalysis. Just what 'Deleuzean' literary criticism would be remains an open question. In *Germinal Life* (1999) Keith Ansell-Pearson uses the work of Deleuze to reread Thomas Hardy and D. H. Lawrence. Ansell-Pearson takes Deleuze's arguments regarding life and creation and finds these themes in novels. Ansell-Pearson does not so much offer a literary *theory* as see the literature as expressive of Deleuze's own readings of Darwin and Bergson: the novels depict a life flowing through and across bodies, 'the extravagant life which in the course of evolution has always exceeded the effort of self-preservation' (Ansell-Pearson 1999: 192). In *Deleuzism* (2000) Ian Buchanan makes more of an attempt to offer a Deleuzean way of reading, rather than just seeing literature as expressive of Deleuze's own beliefs. For Buchanan, taking up Deleuze for literary theory means taking Deleuze's concept of the virtual seriously. There are actual literary texts – such as the novels of Herman Melville – and then the virtual forces or powers that created those texts. 'Metacommentary', according to Buchanan, does not locate texts within historical contexts – such as seeing Shakespeare as a 'Renaissance' author – but it does try to look at the social and political dynamics and *problems* from which texts emerge (Buchanan 2000). Buchanan, with John Marks (2000), has also edited a volume of essays on Deleuze and literature which shows the potential diversity of approaches to Deleuze and literature.

Deleuzean criticism is, though, in its early days. Probably the best place to begin with unpacking what Deleuze means for literary studies is to look at what he *does*: the way he sees Proust as motivated by the *problem* of signs (or of how we see beyond the actual world to what the world, and others, can disclose). In his *Essays: Critical and Clinical* (1997) we can also look at Deleuze's uses of Lawrence, Melville and other writers who make language 'stutter' in order to produce new actualisations from the power of literature. Above all, though, the challenge of 'Deleuzism' is not to repeat what Deleuze *said* but to look at literature as productive of new ways of saying and seeing.

FURTHER READING

Most of Deleuze's works are now in translation. Probably the best place for literature students to begin reading Deleuze is Deleuze's book on Proust, *Proust and Signs*, which also introduces many of Deleuze's important philosophical themes, such as time, the virtual and becoming. From there, it should be easier to cope with Deleuze's collected essays on literature, *Essays: Critical and Clinical,* and Deleuze's book on Kafka with Guattari, *Kafka: Towards a Minor Literature*. Deleuze's early works on philosophers, particularly his book on Hume, *Empiricism and Subjectivity*, are also quite clear and less laden with Deleuze's own idiosyncratic terminology than his later works. Deleuze's major work is *Difference and Repetition*, but this is an encyclopedic work, covering a vast array of authors, topics and terminology. Rather than read the book from cover to cover, a single chapter (such as the third chapter on 'The Image of Thought') will give some idea of the key Deleuzean themes of thought as creation rather than representation. The same reading method applies to the major works he co-authored with Guattari, *Anti-Oedipus* and *A Thousand Plateaus*. Both works cover a huge amount of argument and material, so it is best to decide upon a single section or plateau. The fourth section of *Anti-Oedipus* 'Introduction to Schizo-analysis' and the tenth plateau in *A Thousand Plateaus* on becoming-woman would be good places to start. If there is one book that provides an overview of Deleuze's project, apart from the dense *Difference and*

Repetition, it is his late work with Guattari, *What is Philosophy?*. Here, Deleuze and Guattari offer broad definitions of art, philosophy and science and offer criticisms of the current 'communicational' or market-oriented approach to culture and thinking.

WORKS BY DELEUZE

Deleuze, G. (1973) *Proust and Signs*, trans. R. Howard, London: Allen Lane/Penguin.

A study of the French novelist, Marcel Proust, using the French philosopher Henri Bergson's philosophy of time. Published in French in 1964.

Deleuze, G. (1981) *Francis Bacon: Logique de la Sensation*, Paris: Editions de la Différence.

One of the few works by Deleuze to remain untranslated into English. A study of the twentieth-century artist Francis Bacon.

Deleuze, G. (1983) *Nietzsche and Philosophy*, trans. H. Tomlinson, London: Athlone.

Deleuze offers an anti-humanist reading of Nietzsche, stressing the doctrine of eternal return: life is the affirmation of difference over and over again with no founding origin or external principle.

Deleuze, G. (1984) *Kant's Critical Philosophy: The Doctrine of the Faculties*, trans. H. Tomlinson and B. Habberjam, London: Athlone.

Deleuze reads the enlightenment philosopher against the grain, showing how Kant's theory of the unified subject actually entails a subject of conflict and divergence.

Deleuze, G. (1986) *Cinema 1: The Movement-Image*, trans. H. Tomlinson and B. Habberjam, Minneapolis: University of Minnesota Press.

An exploration of a theory of movement through early cinema.

Deleuze, G. (1987) *Dialogues with Claire Parnet*, trans. H. Tomlinson and B. Habberjam, London: Athlone Press.

As the title indicates, a series of clear and readable dialogues.

Deleuze, G. (1988a) *Spinoza: Practical Philosophy*, trans. R. Hurley, San Francisco: City Lights Books.

A shorter and more accessible study of Spinoza than *Expressionism in Philosophy*.

Deleuze, G. (1988b) *Foucault*, trans. S. Hand, London: Athlone Press.

A difficult study of Deleuze's contemporary Michel Foucault. Important for the distinctions Deleuze draws between his own stress on immanence and monism, and Foucault's sustained dualism.

Deleuze, G. (1988c) *Bergsonism*, trans. C. Boundas, New York: Zone.

Many commentators argue that, along with Nietzsche, Bergson is Deleuze's most important predecessor. Deleuze articulates the importance of difference and the virtual through this study of Bergson.

Deleuze, G. (1989) *Cinema 2: The Time-Image*, trans. H. Tomlinson and R. Galeta, Minneapolis: University of Minnesota Press.

Exploring Bergson, the philosophy of time, modern cinema and the entire problem of philosophy, this book is one of Deleuze's most important. It begins with an overview of the theory of the movement-image before moving on to time.

Deleuze, G. (1990) *The Logic of Sense*, trans. M. Lester, ed. C. V. Boundas, New York: Columbia University Press.

A wide-ranging and difficult study of the problem of meaning or sense ranging from the Stoicism of Ancient Greece to the nonsense literature of Lewis Carroll.

Deleuze, G. (1991) *Empiricism and Subjectivity: An Essay on Hume's Theory of Human Nature*, trans. Constantin V. Boundas, New York: Columbia University Press.

Deleuze's first book, which is also a remarkably clear study of the Scottish enlightenment philosopher, David Hume.

Deleuze, G. (1992) *Expressionism in Philosophy*, trans. M. Joughin, New York: Zone Books.

Deleuze rereads Spinoza through the key notion of immanence, with a conclusion on the relation between Spinoza and Leibniz.

Deleuze, G. (1993) *The Fold: Leibniz and the Baroque*, trans. T. Conley, London: Athlone.

An immensely difficult work that reads the philosopher Leibniz alongside insights from contemporary music and mathematics.

Deleuze, G. (1994) *Difference and Repetition*, trans. P. Patton, New York: Columbia University Press.

This is probably Deleuze's most important work as it directly confronts the problem of difference and concepts of difference. It does, however, require some acquaintance with Deleuze's interventions in philosophy, mathematics and genetics.

Deleuze, G. (1995) *Negotiations 1972–1990*, trans. Martin Joughin, New York: Columbia University Press.

A series of short essays and interviews, with some very readable pieces.

Deleuze, G. (1997) *Essays: Critical and Clinical*, trans. D. W. Smith and M. A. Greco, Minneapolis: University of Minnesota Press.

An inspiring and readable collection of essays on literature and style. The translator's introduction by Daniel Smith is extremely lucid and informative.

WORKS BY DELEUZE AND GUATTARI

Deleuze, G. and Guattari, F. (1983) *Anti-Oedipus: Capitalism and Schizophrenia*, trans. Robert Hurley, Mark Seem and Helen R. Lane, Minneapolis: University of Minnesota Press.

Until recently Deleuze's best-known and most influential work. An attack on conventional psychoanalysis and the industry of therapy in favour of a radical politics of desire.

Deleuze, G. and Guattari, F. (1986) *Kafka: Towards a Minor Literature*, trans. D. Polan, Minneapolis: University of Minnesota Press.

A study of the Czech writer, Franz Kafka, which explores broader questions on the relation between politics, desire and literature.

Deleuze, G. and Guattari, F. (1987) *A Thousand Plateaus: Capitalism and Schizophrenia,* trans. B. Massumi, Minneapolis: University of Minnesota Press.

Even more unconventional than the first volume, *Anti-Oedipus*. Composed in 'plateaus', rather than chapters, with different styles, voices and disciplines interweaving to form a 'rhizome' (a series of productive connections with no centre or foundation).

Deleuze, G. and Guattari, F. (1994) *What is Philosophy?*, trans. H. Tomlinson and G. Burchill, London: Verso.

Written almost as a manifesto, this book stresses the difference of art, philosophy and science – with an emphasis on the *creative* power of thought.

WORKS ON DELEUZE

There have been some important works on Deleuze that have not yet been translated into English. There is also a large number of specialist articles. The list below includes most of the book-length studies in English. Most of these books operate at a relatively advanced level, so it would be advisable to read more of Deleuze's own texts before turning to secondary reading. However, once a good range of Deleuze's work has been covered, these higher-level works of commentary and criticism should prove useful.

Ansell Pearson, K. (ed.) (1997) *Deleuze and Philosophy: The Difference Engineer*, London: Routledge.
    A collection of essays with an emphasis on Deleuze as a philosopher.

Ansell Pearson, K. (1999) *Germinal Life: The Difference and Repetition of Deleuze*, London: Routledge.
    A reading of Deleuze through Bergson and evolutionary theory.

Badiou, A. (2000) *Deleuze: The Clamor of Being*, trans. Louise Burchill, Minneapolis: University of Minnesota Press.
    The French philosopher, Alain Badiou, differentiates his own project from that of Deleuze, with a focus on the question of univocity.

Bogue, R. (1989) *Deleuze and Guattari*, London: Routledge.
    An overview of Deleuze and Guattari's work, but written before their deaths and therefore not inclusive of all their work.

Brusseau, J. (1998) *Isolated Experiences: Gilles Deleuze and the Solitudes of Reversed Platonism*, Albany: State University of New York Press.
    Philosophically sophisticated extension of Deleuze's gesture of reversing Platonism. Some references to literature, such as F. Scott Fitzgerald and Steve Erickson.

Bryden, M. (2001) *Deleuze and Religion*, London: Routledge.
    Looks at Deleuze in relation to questions of theology.

Buchanan, I. (ed.) (1997) *A Deleuzian Century?*, special issue of *The South Atlantic Quarterly* (96: 3)
    A collection of essays from various angles, including literature, feminism and cultural studies.

Buchanan, I. (2000) *Deleuzism: A Metacommentary*, Durham: Duke University Press.

As the title suggests, not so much an introduction as an attempt to think through the implications of Deleuze's work for culture, politics, literature and film.

Buchanan, I. and Colebrook, C. (2000) *Deleuze and Feminist Theory*, Edinburgh: Edinburgh University Press.
A collection of essays from a number of authors relating Deleuze to feminism and film, literature, culture, politics and the future.

Buchanan, I. and Marks, J. (2001) *Deleuze and Literature*, Edinburgh: Edinburgh University Press.
A collection of essays by various authors, with a specific attention to questions of literature.

Boundas, C. V. and Olkowski, D. (eds) (1994) *Deleuze and the Theater of Philosophy*, New York: Routledge.
A collection of essays from a number of writers.

Goodchild, P. (1994) *Gilles Deleuze and the Question of Philosophy*, London: Associated University Presses.
An overview of Deleuze's philosophy.

Goodchild, P. (1996) *Deleuze and Guattari: An Introduction to the Politics of Desire*, London: Sage.
A clear introduction with some good examples of political questions and issues.

Hardt, M. (1993) *Gilles Deleuze: An Apprenticeship in Philosophy*, London: UCL Press.
An inspiring and original assessment of Deleuze's rereading of Henri Bergson and Baruch de Spinoza and its importance for politics.

Holland, E. W. (1993) *Baudelaire and Schizoanalysis: the Sociopoetics of Modernism*, Cambridge: Cambridge University Press.
Reads the French poet Baudelaire through *Anti-Oedipus* rather than Deleuze's work as a whole.

Holland, E. W. (1999) *Deleuze and Guattari's Anti-Oedipus: An Introduction to Schizoanalysis*, London: Routledge.
A specific focus on *Anti-Oedipus* with a clear explanation of its use of the thought of Karl Marx and Georges Bataille.

Kaufman, E. and Heller, K. J. (eds) (1998) *Deleuze and Guattari: New Mappings in Politics, Philosophy and Culture*, Minneapolis: University of Minnesota Press.
Essays by a number of authors on a wide range of issues.

Marks, J. (1998) *Gilles Deleuze: Vitalism and Multiplicity*, London: Pluto Press.

An introduction to Deleuze which places his ideas in context.

Massumi, B. (1992) *A User's Guide to Capitalism and Schizophrenia*, Cambridge, MA.: MIT Press.

Contrary to the title this is not an introductory work. Massumi thinks through and beyond Deleuze and Guattari rather than commenting on or explaining their ideas.

Patton, P. (ed.) (1996) *Deleuze: A Critical Reader*, Oxford: Basil Blackwell.

A collection of essays by major philosophers.

Patton, P. (2000) *Deleuze and the Political*, London: Routledge.

A clear and original account of the implications of Deleuze's philosophy for contemporary politics and political theory.

Rajchman, J. (2000) *The Deleuze Connections*, Cambridge MA: MIT Press.

An advanced overview of the implications of Deleuze's concepts and method.

WORKS CITED

For bibliographic information on works by Deleuze, or by Deleuze and Guattari, see pp. 153–6 in the Further Reading section.

Austen, J. (1972) *Pride and Prejudice*, Harmondsworth: Penguin.

Ansell Pearson, K. (1999) *Germinal Life: The Difference and Repetition of Deleuze*, London: Routledge.

Braidotti, R. (1994), *Nomadic Subjects*, New York: Columbia University Press.

Brontë, C. (1985) *Jane Eyre*, Harmondsworth: Penguin.

Brooke, R. (1970) *The Poetical Works of Rupert Brooke*, ed. G. Keynes, London: Faber and Faber.

Buchanan, I. (2000) *Deleuzism: A Metacommentary*, Durham: Duke University Press.

Buchanan, I. and Marks, J. (eds) (2001) Deleuze and Literature, Edinburgh: Edinburgh University Press.

Carey, P. (1988) *Oscar and Lucinda*, London: Faber.

Carroll, L. (1939) *The Complete Works of Lewis Carroll*, London: The Nonesuch Press.

Coetzee, J. M. (1986) *Foe*, London: Secker & Warburg.

Defoe, D. (1998) *The Life and Strange Surprizing Adventures of Robinson Crusoe, of York, Mariner*, ed. J. D. Crowley, Oxford: Oxford University Press.

DeLillo, D. (1985) *White Noise*, London: Picador.

Dickens, C. (1994) *Great Expectations*, Harmondsworth: Penguin.

Dickinson, E. (1975) *The Complete Works of Emily Dickinson*, ed. T. H. Johnson, London: Faber.

Dostoevsky, F. (1972) *Notes from Underground / The Double*, trans. J. Coulson, Harmondsworth: Penguin.

Eliot, T. S. (1974) *Collected Poems 1909–1962*, London: Faber and Faber.

Ellis, B. E. (1991) *American Psycho*, London: Picador.

Ellis, B. E. (1999) *Glamorama*, New York: Alfred A. Knopf.

Foucault, M. (1972) *The Archaeology of Knowledge and the Discourse on Language*, trans. A. M. Sheridan Smith, New York: Pantheon.

Gatens, M. and Lloyd, G. (1999) *Collective Imaginings: Spinoza Past and Present*, London: Routledge.

Gosse, E. (1970) *Father and Son*, Harmondsworth: Penguin.

Grosz, E. (1994) *Volatile Bodies: Towards a Corporeal Feminism*, Bloomington: Indiana University Press.

Hardt, M. (1993) *Gilles Deleuze: An Apprenticeship in Philosophy*, London: UCL Press.

Hardt, M. and Negri, A. (1994) *Labor of Dionysus*, Minneapolis: University of Minnesota Press.

Holland, E. W. (1993) *Beaudelaire and Schizoanalysis: the Sociopoetics of Modernism*, Cambridge: Cambridge University Press.

Hughes, J. (1997) *Lines of Flight: Reading Deleuze with Hardy, Gissing, Conrad, Woolf*, Sheffield: Sheffield Academic.

James, H. (1965) *The Wings of the Dove*, Harmondsworth: Penguin.

Joyce, J. (1964) *A Portrait of the Artist as a Young Man*, New York: Viking.

Joyce, J. (1977) *The Essential James Joyce*, ed. H. Levin, London : Triad Paladin.

Kafka, F. (1961) *Metamorphosis and Other Stories*, trans. W. and E. Muir, Harmondsworth: Penguin.

Kafka, F. (1925) *The Trial*, trans. W. and E. Muir, London: Gollancz [1937].

Massumi, B. (1996) 'The Autonomy of Affect', in P. Patton (ed.) *Deleuze: A Critical Reader*, Oxford: Basil Blackwell, 217–40.

Massumi, B. (2001) *A Shock to Thought*, New York: Routledge.

Melville, H. (1998) *Moby Dick*, ed. T. Tanner, Oxford: Oxford University Press.

Nietzsche, F. (1882) *The Gay Science: With a Prelude in Rhymes and an Appendix of Songs*, New York: Vintage Books [1974].

Nietzsche, F. (1961) *Thus Spake Zarathustra: A Book for Everyone and No One*, trans. R. J. Hollingdale, Harmondsworth: Penguin.

Patto, P. (2000) *Deleuze and the Political*, London: Routledge.

Rhys, J. (1966) *Wide Sargasso Sea*, Harmondsworth: Penguin [1998].

Rodowick, D. N. (1997) *Gilles Deleuze's Time Machine*, Durham: Duke University Press.

Shaviro, S. (1993) *The Cinematic Body*, Minneapolis: University of Minnesota Press.

Woolf, V. (1931) *The Waves*, London: The Hogarth Press.

INDEX

happiness 15, 17, 19
Hegel, G. W. F. 3
Heidegger, Martin 1, 6
hermeneutics 137
history 2–3, 58, 61–2, 75–6
humanism 55, 82–3, 125–6
Hume, David 3, 63, 87
The Hunger Artist (Kafka) 42
The Hunting of the Snark (Carroll)
  111
Husserl, Edmund 1, 6
hyperreality 98

idealism 79–80
Ideas 52–3, 105–6, 132–3
identity 2–3
ideology 91–102
images 32, 50–3, 73, 128;
  see also movement-image;
  time-image
immanence 74, 76–9, 86–9
impersonal affects 25–6
impersonal memory 33
impersonal perceptions 139–40
indirect discourse 109–12
the infinitive 109–12
inscription 116
inside–outside 74–5, 149
intensities 38–9, 74, 106–9
interests 91–2, 93
interpretive method 47
interpretosis 71, 134–6
intuition 46–7, 48
investments 61, 108–9, 132
irrational cuts 33–4, 53

James, Henry 25
Jane Eyre (Brontë) 120, 121
joy 132
Joyce, James 33, 112–14, 118, 120,
  122
joyous science 19

Kafka, Franz 42, 103, 104, 109–10,
  128, 134, 136, 137–9

Laing, R. D. 5
language: as affect 113; art of
  114–15; deterritorialised 59;
  difference 21; is metaphorical
  17–18; problems presupposed by
  21; proposition form 110–11; the
  real 66; representation 56, 83–4,
  145; as signifier 107–8
libido 140–5
lines of flight 57, 62
literary style (of Deleuze) 13, 14
literary theory 79, 81, 92,
  150–1
literature: and becoming 129–32,
  136–9, 144–5; cinema
  comparison 30–1; empiricism
  84–6; history 62; literary
  character 81–2; majoritarian 117,
  121; memory 33; minor 103–23;
  philosophy's importance
  for 20
logic 14–15
The Logic of Sense (Deleuze) 125
love 17, 84, 86
Lynch, David 39

machines 55–67, 89, 93, 108;
  desiring 62, 81–2
machinic becoming 55
machinic connections 56
majoritarian literature 117, 121
majoritarian man 139
majoritarian modes 104–5
man 139–40, 145
man–woman opposition 104
matter 95
mechanistic being 57
Melville, Herman 133, 136, 150,
  151